MGM STYLE

CEDRIC GIBBONS AND THE ART OF THE GOLDEN AGE OF HOLLYWOOD

HOWARD GUTNER

LYONS PRESS

Guilford, Connecticut

An imprint of The Rowman & Littlefield Publishing Group, Inc.
4501 Forbes Blvd., Ste. 200
Lanham, MD 20706
www.rowman.com

Distributed by NATIONAL BOOK NETWORK

British Library Cataloguing in Publication Information available

Library of Congress Cataloging-in-Publication Data

Names: Gutner, Howard, author.
Title: MGM style : Cedric Gibbons and the art of the golden age of Hollywood /
  Howard Gutner.
Description: Guilford, Connecticut : Lyons Press , [2019] | Includes
  bibliographical references and index.
Identifiers: LCCN 2019012428 (print) | LCCN 2019018505 (ebook) | ISBN
  9781493038589 (e-book) | ISBN 9781493038572 | ISBN
  9781493038572 (hardback : alk. paper) | ISBN 9781493038589 (e-book)
Subjects: LCSH: Gibbons, Cedric, 1895-1960. | Metro-Goldwyn-Mayer. Art
  Department. | Motion picture art directors—California—Los
  Angeles—Biography.
Classification: LCC PN1998.3.G534 (ebook) | LCC PN1998.3.G534 G88 2019
  (print) | DDC 791.4302/5092 [B] —dc23
LC record available at https://lccn.loc.gov/2019012428

This book is for my father and mother, Edward and Irma C. Gutner.

It is dedicated to the hundreds of expert craftspeople who worked anonymously behind the scenes at Metro-Goldwyn-Mayer in order to bring the visions of its art directors to life on the screen.

Whenever someone thinks highly of his own ability as a writer or actor, let him visit any of the sets built for Hollywood productions. He will come away with a somewhat sad conviction that here among the designers, the set dressers, and the builders is exemplified the only honesty Hollywood knows.

—GENE FOWLER,
AMERICAN JOURNALIST, SCREENWRITER, AND DRAMATIST, 1934

CONTENTS

PREFACE

IN 1938 METRO-GOLDWYN-MAYER RELEASED A publicity photograph of the man in charge of the company's art department. Unlike many of the MGM stars who beguiled their public before the still cameras of studio photographers such as George Hurrell and Clarence Sinclair Bull, supervising art director Cedric Gibbons does not look directly into the lens. Nattily attired in an impeccably tailored black suit, Gibbons leans over a set model for *Marie Antoinette*, one of the studio's most expensive pictures up to that time, and, lips pursed, scrutinizes a small model of a proposed set. On Gibbons's left, unit art director William Horning stands with his hands clasped behind his back, intently watching his boss for signs of disapproval. Sharing space on the table with the carefully crafted model are four volumes of reference materials, strategically placed to suggest the painstaking research that went into the set's design.

While this photo was intended for newspapers and periodicals and not the glossy fan magazines that were instrumental in crafting and maintaining a star's popularity, it nevertheless goes a long way toward establishing an image both for MGM and its supervising art director. It is an image that, viewed more than eighty years after it was taken, still summons the aura of a man whose panache and rigorous attention to detail gave MGM productions their distinctive, instantly recognizable sheen. And it reverberates, too, with the recognition Gibbons had already received in both architectural journals and the more popular press, and the power that it had conferred upon him: "A portentous star rising on the decorating horizon," gushed *Collier's* in 1933. "There is probably no other designer in Hollywood who has had a longer and wider range of experience than Cedric Gibbons," wrote *Theater Arts Monthly* in October 1937.

Ralph Flint, writing in the magazine *Creative Art*, concurred. "I must refer to him as the dean of the Hollywood art directors," he wrote. "Cedric Gibbons deserve[s] more than a passing salute, since he is one of the real focal points of the studio." Flint concluded that next to studio head Louis B. Mayer and Irving Thalberg, executive vice president in charge of production, Gibbons was the most powerful person in the MGM hierarchy. He certainly lasted longer than any other executive at the studio and, as a result, had more of an ongoing and long-term impact on the look of the MGM films than any other single individual in the company's history. Indeed, his influence and personal taste often cast a wider net, extending beyond the studio's gates in Culver City and into the editorial boardrooms of magazines such as *House and Garden*, *House Beautiful*, and even *Harper's Bazaar* and *Vogue*.

Gibbons was already an art director at the Goldwyn Studios when it merged with the Metro company and Louis B. Mayer Productions and became incorporated as Metro-Goldwyn-Mayer in 1924. A year later, Mayer tapped him to become the head of the art department at the new studio, a position Gibbons held for thirty-one years until ill health forced him to retire in 1956. Although he obviously did not personally create the sets for all of the films MGM produced during this period, he did have complete control over department personnel, the assignment of tasks, final design decisions, and the attribution of credit.

Nominated for the Academy Award an astonishing thirty-nine times, Gibbons received the Oscar, which he was also credited with designing, for art direction on eleven occasions, for *The Bridge of San Luis Rey* (1929), *The Merry Widow* (with Fredric Hope, 1934), *Pride and Prejudice* (1940, b&w, with Paul Groesse), *Blossoms in the Dust* (1941, color, with Urie McCleary and Edwin B. Willis), *Gaslight* (1944, b&w, with William Ferrari, Edwin B. Willis, and Paul Huldschinsky), *The Yearling* (1946, color, with Paul Groesse and Edwin B. Willis), *Little Women* (1949, color, with Paul Groesse, Edwin B. Willis, and Jack D. Moore), *An American in Paris* (1951, color, with Preston Ames, Edwin B. Willis, and F. Keogh Gleason), *The Bad and the Beautiful* (1952, b&w, with Edward C. Carfagno, Edwin B. Willis, and F. Keogh Gleason), *Julius Caesar* (1953, b&w, with Edward C. Carfagno, Edwin B. Willis, and Hugh Hunt), and *Somebody Up There Likes Me* (1956, b&w, with Malcolm Brown, Edwin B. Willis, and F. Keogh Gleason).

The list is striking for the breadth of genres it covers: musicals, melodramas, historical epics, and literary adaptations. But what exactly was the "MGM style," and how was it articulated in films as disparate in content and mood as, say, *The Merry Widow* and *Gaslight*? How did Gibbons go about implementing it through three successive decades? And how much input did he really bestow on the films for which he shared credit with the unit art director assigned to the production? For the 1938 publicity photograph has a dark undertone—one that, to the modern observer, suggests a tyrannical overlord concerned with his own image above all else, who did very little actual work except to review the labor of those who reported to him. It is an image that has superseded many of Gibbons's accomplishments, as some contemporary assessments describe an aloof supervisor arriving on the lot in his Duesenberg, carefully removing calfskin gloves as he proceeds to his spacious office without a word to anyone on his staff. But this was hardly the case.

Preston Ames, who arrived at MGM in 1936 and later worked on musicals such as *An American in Paris* and *The Band Wagon* (1953), notes simply that "the art department at Metro was what it was because Cedric Gibbons created it."

What Gibbons created, and was instrumental in building, had its genesis in the physical lot where he had been working since 1918; for when the Metro-Goldwyn-Mayer merger transpired, the new studio took over the Goldwyn lot in Culver City. D. W. Griffith, Mack Sennett, and Thomas H. Ince had actually built it when they formed the Triangle Film Corporation in 1915, and Goldwyn had taken it over three years later.

This main lot, later known simply as Lot 1, was like a city within a city, with its own police and fire departments, telegraph and post office, water tower and well. At the west end of the property, a large concrete tank was built and used for underwater scenes and for the special effects needed in such sea pictures as *Mutiny on the Bounty* (1935) and *Captains Courageous* (1937). On the forty acres that surrounded this tank, Gibbons and his art directors built the first large outdoor sets at MGM—a harbor community used in *Anna Christie* (1930) and *Tugboat Annie* (1932) and a large Indonesian waterfront village for *Red Dust* (1932).

In 1935–36 Gibbons supervised a major expansion of the backlot, which would eventually cover close to 187 acres by the early 1940s. On one hundred of those acres, in what later became known as Lots 2 and 3, Gibbons and his associates constructed the villages, towns, streets, squares, and edifices that later appeared in hundreds of films, and whose mixed architecture stood in for army camps and waterfront docks, modern-day Manhattan and Dickensian London, ancient China and eighteenth-century France.

One of the first realized outdoor sets was "Small Town Square," built by Gibbons and William Horning for Fritz Lang's first American film, *Fury*, in 1936. Although part of the set was burned for a climactic scene in the film, its malt shop, dry-goods store, courthouse, and park were later restored. Throughout the late 1930s and continuing into the 1950s, Judy Garland, Ann Miller, June Allyson, and Eleanor and Jane Powell usually skipped off to the Great White Way from this small-town re-creation in films such as *Presenting Lily Mars* (1943) and *Cynthia* (1947). Literally warbling "Take Me to Broadway," Bobby Van transforms into a human pogo stick and covers the length of the entire set for a number in *Small Town Girl* (1953). The smoky evacuation scenes in *Raintree County* (1956) were filmed here, and, as late as 1962, artificial snow covered the street for the film version of Tennessee Williams's *Period of Adjustment*. In 1944, directly behind this square, Gibbons and associate art director Lemuel Ayres designed a set for Vincente Minnelli's *Meet Me in St. Louis* that would later become known as "St. Louis Street." A good block long, the curving avenue contained eight three-story Victorian mansions and was used again and again for more than twenty years, redressed and even rented by other studios for such films as *All Fall Down* (1961) and *Summer and Smoke* (1962).

The focal point of the MGM backlot, however, was to be found on three outdoor sets, all of which were built just before or during the 1935–36 expansion. "Wimpole Street" was built for the 1934 film version of the Rudolf Besier play *The Barretts of Wimpole Street*, which starred Norma Shearer and Fredric March. It consisted of two sides of a nineteenth-century British square, gaslit with four-story, garret-topped buildings fronting on a park enclosed by a high wrought iron fence. It was later used for brooding night scenes in both *Gaslight* and *The Picture of Dorian Gray* (1945) and was still in use in the 1960s when Minnelli shot scenes here for *The Four Horsemen of the Apocalypse*. "Waterfront Street" was originally built for *A Tale of Two Cities* in 1935. Its French heritage enabled it to be used prominently in such films as *Madame Bovary* (1949), *An American in Paris*, *The Last Time I Saw Paris* (1954), and *Les Girls* (1959).

Encompassing these two sets were three other distinctive areas known as "Brownstone Street," "Fifth Avenue," and "Eastside Street." These were among the oldest standing sets at MGM, and over time alleys were cut through the various sections so that the buildings of one street were joined to the others. This created a large area that covered approximately ten acres, and it could be used to represent almost any kind of urban

"Wimpole Street" was constructed for the 1934 version of *The Barretts of Wimpole Street*. Ten years later, one of the townhome fronts on this nineteenth-century British square would serve as Ingrid Bergman's home in *Gaslight*.

environment. The entire area was rigged with a network of fifty-foot catwalks that allowed a whole street, or a section of it, to be enclosed in canvas for shooting night scenes during the day. Margaret O'Brien got lost on these streets in *Journey for Margaret* (1942). Joan Crawford trudged home to her tenement apartment here in *Our Blushing Brides* (1930) and *Mannequin* (1938). Clark Gable and Jean Harlow reported for work in *Wife vs.*

Secretary (1936). And many heroines trod its pavements after leaving Small Town Square for the big city. It stood in for Broadway in the Broadway Melody series, Chicago in *In the Good Old Summertime* (1949), and even for Hollywood itself. Gene Kelly danced and sang down one of its rain-washed streets in *Singin' in the Rain* (1953).

In its lighthearted way *Singin' in the Rain* captured some of the panic that had swept through MGM and all the other studios at the dawn of the sound era in 1928. Early in that landmark musical, Kelly and Donald O'Connor walk through a facsimile of one of the glass stages used during the silent era, with seven or eight films in production under one

"Eastside Street," one of the oldest standing sets at MGM, was built to represent any major urban area. It is seen here soon after it was completed in 1936. In 1952, Gene Kelly and Stanley Donen would stage Kelly's iconic *Singin' in the Rain* number here.

Two aerial photographs of MGM's Lot 2, taken in the late 1930s.

roof, often side by side. These glass stages would soon give way to more than twenty-five sound stages by the end of the 1930s, four of them built in an orgy of construction during a three-month period from August to October 1928. As Scott Eyman wrote, "Grass was ripped up, magnolias and willow trees chopped down. Where there had been flowers, there was now asphalt. A sylvan atmosphere was converted into something industrial." In short, a factory was born. Stage 6, the tallest sound stage in the world for decades, contained a proscenium arch for staging theatrical extravaganzas on the order of *Dancing Lady* (1933), *The Great Ziegfeld* (1936), *Ziegfeld Girl* (1941), and *Broadway Melody of 1940*. Stage 15 was, until the 1960s, the largest sound stage in the world, covering an area of 41,985 square feet with a ceiling height of forty feet.

Within these sound stages, Gibbons and his collaborators devised and constructed many interior sets that, particularly in the 1930s and early '40s, became a testing ground for experiments in modern architecture and interior design. Inspired by the work of Le Corbusier and the Bauhaus masters, as well as the 1925 Exposition Internationale des Arts Décoratifs et Industriels Modernes in Paris and Frank Lloyd Wright's experiments with open planning, Gibbons championed the notion that movie décor should move beyond the commercial framework of the popular cinema: "If imagination is permitted to soar in contemporary settings," he wrote in 1929, "we may look for a setting which in itself will be as completely modern as is modern painting and sculpture."

Liberated from the constraints that an architectural firm might encounter, such as specific sites, the laws of nature, a dwindling post-1929 economy, and the tastes of individual clients, Gibbons's preoccupation with geometrical form and movement within a set began as early as 1927, in films such as *London after Midnight* and *The Masks of the Devil*, and became fully evident a year later in *Our Dancing Daughters* and its sequel, *Our Modern Maidens* (1929). Abetted by such talented designers as Alexander Toluboff, Merrill Pye, and Richard Day, Gibbons used the narrative momentum of commercial film to propel and help "sell" the idea of modernism to a public and popular press that was still somewhat intransigent in its taste.

His success can be measured in the editorial boardrooms of publications such as *Harper's Bazaar*. In 1928, before the release of *Our Dancing Daughters*, the magazine published the article "A Day in a Modern Apartment," offering a lighthearted look at the supposed travails of living amid modern décor: "Why, in some houses you can actually tell which [*sic*] is the bed. That is another old-fashioned idea. It's much more amusing to guess what each piece of furniture is." Later that year, the magazine's editors were lamenting that "few [houses] are inhabited by individuals who feel that their homes should be as asymmetrical, efficient, and beautiful as the motors they ride in, the ships they sail in. May their numbers increase."

Increase they did, as throughout the 1930s and into the 1940s, the MGM art department received literally thousands of letters asking for floor plans as well as photographs of Norma Shearer's country house and city apartment in *The Women* (1939) or Joan Crawford's writer's retreat in *When Ladies Meet* (1941), just as the costume department received requests for the costumes these actresses wore in their films. "A set," Gibbons wrote in the early 1930s, "can of itself tell a whole story. To design it, one must study the characters in the play, and try to personify them in their settings. Then one must examine the dramatic action and see that no detail in the set might catch the eye and detract from the story. The ideal setting so perfectly blends itself with the action of the drama that one enhances the other."

The slogan of the art department at MGM was "You write it, we will make it for you." And when in 1938 Cedric Gibbons was asked by author Stephen Watts to define just what the significance of an art director is in a film studio, he jokingly replied that he is the man "who makes everyone's dreams come true."

George Cukor, a film director who made excellent use of the MGM art department's vast resources for decades and who later worked outside the studio system, would probably have agreed with Gibbons, although he saw the benefits of both methods. "You're on your own [today], which in a sense is a very good thing. You have to fend for yourself. Some of that can be very stimulating. But I'll tell you what is sad. The studios had the most wonderful technicians. They created seventy-five years of absolute technical perfection. Well, these people have retired and died. I'm sure there are all kinds of new ones, but the studio people were of a dazzling brilliance. Also, they had something in their spirit which was wonderful. They had a stake in the picture; they wanted the picture to be right; and they were with you all the time."

Making dreams come true.

CHAPTER ONE

THE BUILDER'S SON

THIS IS THE WEST, SIR," A REPORTER TELLS JIMMY Stewart near the end of John Ford's western *The Man Who Shot Liberty Valance*. "When the legend becomes fact, print the legend."

Shortly after the end of World War I, when Cedric Gibbons arrived in Los Angeles, Southern California was about as far west as you could go. And Gibbons's own legend was just beginning to evolve. He would husband it assiduously throughout the 1930s and '40s. Each morning the process would begin anew when his secretary at MGM, Norma Jean Wright, brought in his mail along with the Los Angeles newspapers. Scanning the trades first, Gibbons would then read the gossip columns, in particular those that appeared in the *Los Angeles Times* and the *Los Angeles Herald-Examiner*. The *Times* was the home base for Jimmie Fidler, whose column "Jimmie Fidler in Hollywood" was also syndicated in 187 other newspapers across the country. In 1941 Errol Flynn had accosted the gossip columnist at the Mocambo nightclub on Sunset Boulevard and struck him for, in his words, "telling too many lies about the motion picture business." And on June 21, 1941, a small item in Jimmie Fidler's column caught Cedric Gibbons's eye: "Pat Dane asking Slapsy Maxie's band to play a Hawaiian war chant, while boyfriend Cedric Gibbons, not long back from Honolulu, demonstrates a native dance."

Cedric Gibbons in 1910, two years before he enrolled in the Art Students League.

Slapsy Maxie's was a nightclub where a certain stratum of Hollywood society flirted with the underworld. Prizefighter-turned-character actor Max Rosenbloom was the front man and ostensible owner of the establishment, but most people knew that mobster Mickey Cohen held the purse strings. That this brief item in a Hollywood gossip column may or may not have been fabricated—or was at the very least a gross exaggeration of what actually took place—was not important. It did not fit the image Gibbons wanted to polish and protect, and he responded immediately in a letter written the same day the story appeared:

> Dear Jimmy [*sic*] Fidler,
>
> Fun's fun, but for the love of God will you have a little respect for my gray hairs and years—and grant me just a small amount of decorum?
>   I write you this because in the first place I have never been to Slapsy Maxie's, nor do I know any Hawaiian dances—or any other kind of dances. And in the second place, to be quite honest and sincere, it makes me very unhappy to be made to appear ridiculous. I would hate to think that was your intention. I would be grateful if you could set the record straight.

Fidler did make amends, and Gibbons responded by telling Fidler that perhaps he overreacted, melodramatically despairing that he must be losing his sense of humor. But "setting the record straight" was of prime importance to Cedric Gibbons, although in some respects it was a record he had edited and created for himself out of whole cloth. Official MGM biographies of their supervisory art director (more than one was made public over the course of his thirty-two-year career at the studio) effortlessly blended selected facts and half-truths that were interwoven with outright fiction, each version slightly altered and blurred to keep pace with the tempo of the times in which it was released.

The popular press used the information in these press releases as signposts, disseminating "facts" to the public that would inform and lend authority to Gibbons's designs for the studio. "He studied painting in his youth," wrote R. R. Crisler in the February 6, 1938, edition of the *New York Times*, "but absorbed architecture from association with his father and grandfather, who were both architects (his grandfather finished St. Patrick's Cathedral). He has grown up with the motion picture industry, beginning in 1912 at the Edison Studio, where he designed sets for Mrs. Patrick Campbell and Mrs. Leslie Carter."

Five years earlier, in *Collier's*, Betty Thornley Stuart, in an overview of motion picture set design from its earliest days to the present, compared Gibbons's arrival on the Hollywood scene to a cosmic event, calling him "a star that had first seen the light in Dublin in 1893. Its name in the flesh is Cedric Gibbons. Having traveled in England and France, Italy and Germany to study art, costumes, furniture and decorations, the future luminary decided to become a painter and came to New York in 1912. Almost at once the movies caught his attention. His enthusiasm for reform was such that he pulled off a job as art director for the old Thomas Edison Studio at Bedford Park, New York, went from there to the Goldwyn Organization, and moved with the firm to California."

Scan the internet and you will still see bits and pieces of these articles and press releases, distilled and perpetuated across the decades like specks of memory from a press agent's dream and accepted by many as fact. In reality, however, while Gibbons did work at the Edison Studios located at 199th Street and Oliver Place in Bronx, New York, he worked primarily as a set dresser and as an assistant to art director Hugo Ballin, and he couldn't have designed sets for Mrs. Patrick Campbell and Mrs. Carter. Campbell made six films, the first in 1920, two years after the Edison Studios had closed its doors. Mrs. Carter made three silent films between 1915 and 1916, produced respectively by the George Kleine Company, Tiffany Productions, and a film company in Great Britain. But Mrs. Carter, known as the "American Sarah Bernhardt," had passed away in November 1937, so when the *Times* article appeared early in 1938, her name was fresh in the public's collective imagination. Declaring that the young Cedric Gibbons had designed sets for these two legendary theatrical figures gave his own evolving legend distinction, dramatic effect, and a certain gravitas.

A fair number of sources other than *Collier's* still claim that Gibbons was born in Dublin. In fact, Cedric Gibbons was born at 76 Rush Street in Brooklyn, New York, on March 22, 1890. He was baptized soon afterward at the Church of St. Peter and Paul, in the Williamsburg section of Brooklyn, by Reverend Sylvester Malone. His birth certificate read "Austin Cedric Gibbons," but from a very young age his parents called him "Cedric," in all likelihood to distinguish him from his father. And the real story of his youth is, in actual fact, more remarkable than any Hollywood press agent's puffery.

Gibbons's father, Austin Patrick Gibbons, was born in Liverpool, England, of Irish parents, on August 31, 1866. When he was three years old, Austin moved to the United States with his parents, Patrick and Mary Kerrigan Gibbons. The Gibbons family emigrated at the tail end of an Irish diaspora initiated by the catastrophic potato famine that had caused rampant starvation in Ireland. Like many immigrant groups before them, the Irish faced daunting problems when they landed in New York City. Perhaps the most crippling was a glaring lack of employable skills. The majority of these immigrants were itinerant farmers escaping a calamitous natural disaster. Patrick Gibbons would have faced a bleak employment picture and an unwelcoming populace if not for one thing in his favor: he was not a farmer but a builder, plying his trade in Liverpool. Gibbons had heard stories about the building boom in America that had attended the end of the Civil War. He was certain that a fresh start in New York City would enable him to provide for his family in a manner that would never have been possible in Liverpool.

The odds, however, were against him. Employers in the United States, throughout the mid- and late nineteenth century, often advertised with "No Irish Need Apply" signs. Irish women, when they were able to find work, almost always labored as domestics and scullery maids. They were stereotyped in the popular press and in the public's mind as "Biddies," short for Bridget, a popular Irish girl's name. In 1854 the *Chicago Post* had editorialized, "The Irish fill our prisons, our poor houses. Scratch a convict or a pauper, and the chances are that you tickle the skin of an Irish Catholic. Putting them on a boat and sending them home would end crime in this country."

But Patrick Gibbons was not about to be sent home. Before departing he had contacted cousins already in New York and had arranged living quarters for his wife and young son on Manhattan's Lower East Side. And there was one other factor in his favor that he hoped would turn the ironic phrase "luck of the Irish" on its head. The cornerstone of the new St. Patrick's Cathedral had been laid on the site of the old Saint John's Church on August 15, 1858. It was a mammoth building project. The boundaries of the church would extend from Fifth to Madison Avenues and Fiftieth to Fifty-First Streets. Construction of the new cathedral had progressed rapidly until it was interrupted by the Civil War and the need for additional funding. The work accelerated in 1868 and lasted through the 1870s, until the cathedral was completed in 1878. Patrick Gibbons was just one of many builders hired to help complete the Gothic structure. He started work just a few short weeks after his arrival in the spring of 1869. He was not, however, employed as an architect. Patrick Gibbons labored in construction his entire life.

Homeschooled by his mother Mary, Austin Gibbons later recalled visiting construction sites with his father and eventually accompanying him to work as a trainee on a wide variety of different construction jobs when he reached his teens. In 1889 he married Veronica Fitzpatrick, when he was twenty-six and she was barely seventeen. On their marriage certificate, Austin listed his occupation as "builder."

Cedric was their first child, soon followed by Veronica Gibbons, named for her mother, on October 24, 1892, and Eliot Shaw Gibbons, their third and last child, on October 4, 1894. All three children were born at 76 Rush Street, the home of their maternal grandparents, Charles and Anna Fitzpatrick. Since their marriage, Austin and his wife had lived with her parents. The house on Rush Street was located only blocks from the Wallabout Channel, site of the US Navy Yard. In 1890 the ill-fated USS *Maine* was launched from the Yard.

Along with his brother and sister, young Cedric was homeschooled by his mother, just as his father had been. Before the birth of her firstborn, Veronica had worked as a biddy in Brooklyn Heights in order to augment her husband's income. Austin moved from job to job, like his father Patrick, and the prospect of unemployment for prolonged lengths of time was always an unforeseen and unwelcome possibility. Veronica was a warm and nurturing presence in the household, and while she was happy over the prospect of spending more time with her children, the loss of income meant that Austin and his wife had to continue living with her parents for the foreseeable future.

Austin naturally assumed that both of his sons would follow him into the construction trade, and when Cedric was still a boy, he began accompanying his father to building sites. Construction was one of Brooklyn's burgeoning industries, and during Cedric's childhood, the last decade of the nineteenth century, the rural character of Brooklyn began to vanish quickly. In 1898, eight years after his birth, it joined four other boroughs (Queens, Manhattan, the Bronx, and Staten Island) to become the city of Greater New York. A series of transportation improvements followed, culminating with the opening of the first subway line tunneled under the East River in 1908. It had been preceded years earlier by the openings of both the Williamsburg Bridge and the Manhattan Bridge. By the time Cedric entered his early teens, Brooklyn had evolved into one of the leading producers of manufactured goods in the nation, and the areas located at the base of each of the new bridges bustled with gas refineries, slaughterhouses, ironworks, sweatshops, and factories that produced everything from clocks to cigars. The excitement in the area was palpable.

Further inland, architects such as Rudolf Daus, John Glover, and Frank Helmle were quickly changing the face of the new borough. The Brooklyn Armory, on Hansen Place, began to rise on April 18, 1891, with a formal ceremony that included a parade. On September 14, 1895, the P. J. Carlin construction company broke ground for the west wing of the Brooklyn Museum. The previous year, Daus's enlargement of the Brooklyn Hall of

Records Building had debuted with much fanfare. Austin Gibbons worked on the construction of both the armory and the museum, and many years later Cedric recalled how magical it was to see a building rise from a hole in the ground, transforming everything around it, altering the very complexion of the neighborhood in which it was built. At a very early age, he became acutely aware of the power of architecture.

In the interviews Gibbons granted during his long tenure at MGM, he mostly avoided talking about his formative years or any formal training he had received. He did maintain that he learned the principles of architecture by working as an apprentice at his father's office. Yet he was never quoted directly, and he never expounded to any journalist on the kinds of projects his father worked on and precisely what he had learned while working at his firm. He simply never disputed or tried to rectify what was dispersed as a fact in his studio biography. And sometime after 1900, Austin Gibbons did open his own office, in a small, seven-story structure on West Twenty-Second Street in Manhattan. It stood in the shadow of the soon-to-be completed Flatiron building.

Gibbons's firm was, in essence, what most people today would consider a contracting business. It could not conceivably compete with firms such as McKim, Mead and White, D. H. Burnham and Company, and Wentworth and Goodhue, whose designs were transforming the New York skyline. But the five boroughs that made up New York City also needed new, modest homes and garages built in response to the growing immigrant workforce and population. Also, remodeling both the exteriors and interiors of private homes was a popular project for many people at this time. By the late 1890s it became more common for middle-class homes to have electricity, telephones, and indoor plumbing. As an experienced builder, these were projects at which the elder Gibbons excelled.

It spoke to Gibbons's success in the field that when his eldest son was seventeen, the office moved to a larger space on Madison Avenue between Fifty-Eighth and Fifty-Ninth Streets. The site now abounds with luxury retailers whose brand names are known across the globe, but at the turn of the twentieth century the neighborhood was still home to a number of middle-class families, and Yorkville, with its large German and Irish immigrant populations, was not very far uptown. With the success of his business, Austin Gibbons was able to move his family out of his parents-in-law's home and into their own row house on Hooper Street in Brooklyn, about three blocks southwest of the house on Rush Street. It was a source of pride for Austin that he was finally able to support his family through his own endeavors, and a culmination of the dream his father Patrick carried with him when he first set foot on American soil.

Working in a firm responsible for the day-to-day supervision of a construction site and the management of vendors and tradespeople offered young Cedric an unparalleled opportunity—the chance to learn all the diverse aspects of the trade as opposed to concentrating, and ultimately specializing in, one specific facet of the operation. He would have started as an apprentice draftsman, working to generate detailed drawings of a structure or renovation project in order to ensure that all parts of the work under construction matched the builder's or architect's specifications.

Architectural drafters have to create drawings that are very precise and easy to understand, as an error in the drawing will be reflected in the finished product. There has to be a clear-cut understanding of the building's elevation, its measurements, and the overall layout. Long before software programs and architectural CAD images were available, Cedric learned to create architectural drawings according to a set of specific conventions that included particular views (floor plan, section, elevation), units of measurement and scales, and annotation and cross-referencing. He also became familiar with how space could be employed in various and, sometimes, unusual ways. The knowledge and skill Gibbons acquired during this period was invaluable in later years when planning and arranging the environment of a motion picture set and assessing and critiquing the work of the art directors he employed at MGM.

Unfortunately, however, his apprenticeship did not last long. The entire Gibbons household was thrown into turmoil when, on April 15, 1910, Cedric's mother Veronica died suddenly after a short illness. The cause was renal failure brought about by acute nephritis due to a kidney stone infection. She was thirty-eight years old.

Cedric was extremely close to Veronica. Due to the fact that he had been homeschooled, Cedric had few childhood friends other than his siblings and the other members of his immediate family. Even though he had just turned twenty when Veronica passed and was no longer a child, it was a severe blow. What transpired afterward was very nearly unbearable. Overwhelmed by grief and incapable of dealing with his loss, Austin Gibbons left his children emotionally, and just months after his wife's death he deserted the family. Like a character in a Dickens novel felled by fate and ill fortune, Cedric's life and career possibilities were upended, and he was left with the responsibility of caring for his two younger siblings along with grandparents who were now well along in years. His situation was a far cry from the web of fantasy spun by MGM publicity. There were no private tutors and no trips to Europe to study "art, costumes, furniture and decorations," as reported in *Collier's*. His father's business was sold to pay back taxes, and the three Gibbons children moved back with their maternal grandparent, who still lived in the house on Rush Street.

In a strange coda to this story, Cedric's father suddenly reappeared in his children's lives in 1928. He was living in Chicago at 76 East Elm Street under the name Robert Errol. Why he changed his name remains unclear, but it may have been to escape his creditors. The younger Gibbons sent his father money from time to time, and one of his letters suggests that he may not have been entirely out of touch with his children from the moment he left them. In a letter dated January 17, 1929, and sent to Gibbons in care of MGM, Errol wrote to his oldest son, "If you have any recent photos of yourself, Cunning (Veronica) and Eliot, I should like to have them. I have one of Cunning when she was married and some of Eliot when he was about fourteen years old but none since and am naturally curious to see how he looks now." In this same letter, he tells Cedric that he has applied for a patent on a fireproof metal window that obviates the necessity of a man donning a harness in order to clean the outskirts of a sash. He closes the letter by telling Cedric, "Wouldn't it be ironic if at the later [*sic*] end of my day I really hit upon something that put me on easy street?"

Cedric began sending his father one hundred dollars a week by the mid-1930s, and in 1938 he began to arrange a trip to Chicago to see him. He also wanted to take his father back with him to Los Angeles. But late in 1937 Errol developed kidney problems that soon became serious. Both Cedric and his sister were able to see him before he passed, on June 22, 1938. On July 22 a friend of Errol's wrote to Cedric, "I am so glad that you saw your father in Chicago. It meant more to him than you could possibly know from any response on his part. Certainly your attentions, and those of your sister, made his last months very happy indeed."

Cedric had begun a hardscrabble existence after his father's desertion in 1910, working most of the time as a builder, as his grandfather and father had done, and moving from job to job. Luckily Cedric's youth and robust physical appearance often made it easy for him to score construction jobs in a field that demanded physical prowess. But now, due to a lack of funds, he was forced to abandon his plans to study architecture at the university level.

Yet Cedric would not let this setback define him. He burned with ambition and spent the next two years attempting to map out a future for himself. He had decided that he would somehow follow his father's lead, moving from the manual labor of construction into a field where he could somehow use his interests in drawing, painting, and architecture.

In 1912 Cedric was able to enroll part-time at the Art Students League of New York. While it did not offer courses in architecture, this decision would eventually point Cedric on his own career path. The League had been founded in 1875 by a group of artists who had begun to chafe under the rigid guidelines of the National Academy of Design, then the leading art school in the United States. In the years after the Civil War, many young artists were falling under the influence of recent developments in the European art world, and they soon felt that the Academy's instruction was too conservative. Initially opened on the top floor of a building at the corner of Fifth Avenue and Sixteenth Street in Manhattan, classes at the League were conducted in one half of a small office space. By the time Gibbons enrolled in 1912, the school had moved to its present location on West Fifty-Seventh Street, between Seventh Avenue and Broadway.

Since its inception, the Art Students League had offered flexible schedules along with reasonable prices, giving it broad appeal to both professionals and amateurs alike. There have never been any degree programs or grades. During his time there, the League would meld Gibbons's life and work experience, transforming not only his artistic sense but also influencing his understanding about how an enterprise dedicated to creativity could be organized and implemented. The League began as—and continues to be—a collection of studios, each one autonomous and directed by the creative authority and counsel of an individual instructor, without interference from the administration. It was just such an operation that Cedric Gibbons would put into practice at MGM, ensuring that the art directors in his employ were able to choose from among a wide range of modes of expression, with himself as creative authority, and with little or no interference from anyone else in the MGM hierarchy.

Gibbons's attendance at the Art Students League was sporadic. He began, as almost every student at the League did at that time, with an introductory course in antiques that focused on drawing from plaster statuary. It later included live models both draped and undraped. Still working as a builder during the day, Gibbons took classes at night, and then added anatomy and life drawing classes to his schedule. He abruptly ceased attending classes in March 1913 due to a lack of funds, only to begin again eighteen months later, enrolling in a life-drawing course. And when in attendance, he was continually looking for contacts and opportunities that would help lead him to a career.

George Bridgman, who was Gibbons's instructor for all the courses he took at the League, was one early contact. It was Bridgman who arranged for him to obtain a Merit

Scholarship, which paid Gibbons's tuition until he left the school. He recalled years later that Gibbons was always concerned with "proper balance within a frame, moving props and subjects until his aesthetic sense was satisfied." During his last months as a student, he moved to Manhattan, occupying the top floor of a row house on Thirty-Fourth Street across from Macy's Department Store. In the teens the Herald Square area was still a theatrical hub in New York City, and it pulsed with life. Less than a block west, the new Pennsylvania Station, which opened in 1910, was the site of almost ceaseless activity, as passengers fanned out day and night between the six Doric columns that framed its entrance. "The voice of time remained aloof and unperturbed," wrote Thomas Wolfe of Penn Station, "a drowsy and eternal murmur below the immense and distant roof."

It was under this immense and distant roof that Cedric would stroll with his sketch pad on warm summer nights. It is easy to surmise why he was attracted to the gargantuan building and its flying buttresses, which seemed to leap from the walls like fountain spray. Penn Station must have appealed to Gibbons for a multitude of reasons: the commanding beauty of its Beaux Arts design, the logistics of constructing an edifice that required the demolition of more than five hundred buildings and the removal of three million cubic yards of soil and bedrock, and the play of shadows and light upon plaster and stone, changing the viewer's perceptions minute by minute. The latter would not be lost on him when he began his career in motion pictures.

It was during these last months at the League, however, that Gibbons had his first actual experience with motion picture set design. Maurice Tourneur was a French director who had moved to New York City to work for William A. Brady's World Film Corporation, where he directed several important early feature-length films. Before long Tourneur was a respected figure in American film and a founding member of the East Coast chapter of the Motion Picture Directors Association. As the feature film evolved in the midteens, Tourneur and his team, which included art director Ben Carré, coupled exceptional technological skill with unique pictorial and architectural sensibilities in their productions, giving their films a visual distinctiveness that met with critical acclaim.

In an interview with silent-film historian Kevin Brownlow, conducted in 1980 for *Sight and Sound*, Carré recalled designing a set for Tourneur's film *Trilby* (1916), which depicted an art class. "I duplicated the studio of Jules Adler in Paris, where I went to have my paintings criticized. To have the atmosphere of a painting class, somebody told the assistant director to approach the Art Center School [i.e., the Art Students League] of New York on 57th Street. We got at least 16 students, and after the scene was taken they were all given still pictures. I got one, and when I saw it again, years later, I recognized Cedric Gibbons!"

The set had been built at production facilities in Fort Lee, New Jersey, where the World Film Corporation rented space from Paragon Studios. The students were picked up in open touring cars in front of the school and spent two days filming in Fort Lee. Gibbons never recorded how he felt working on a film set for the first time, but it is known that he begged George Bridgman for a chance to be included in the group of sixteen students. Soon after this experience, Cedric met an artist who would have a profound influence on his work and indeed provide him, some years later, with the opportunity to meld his professional interests.

Hugo Ballin was born in New York in 1879. Eleven years older than Gibbons, he had had a privileged upbringing. His art education began when he was only seven years old, studying at the studio of figure and portrait painter Wyatt Eaton, one of the founding members of the Society of American Artists. The Society had been formed in 1877 by another group of artists who felt the conservative National Academy of Design no longer adequately met their needs, and in this it was much like the Art Students League. On Eaton's advice Ballin enrolled at the Art Students League in 1903, winning a scholarship for composition and, later, the Shaw Prize, which was given by the National Academy of Design for American figure painting. Ballin used the award money to travel extensively in Europe, ultimately studying fresco painting in Rome. He then returned to New York, where for two years he was an instructor at the League.

By the time Ballin came back to the League as a guest lecturer at the invitation of George Bridgman, he was a member of the National Institute of Arts and Letters and the Architectural League. His entry in the 1910–11 edition of *Who's Who in America* stated that at the age of thirty, Ballin was "weighted down with the gold in the medals won by his talent."

As far as Gibbons was concerned, Ballin's lectures at the school were auspicious, for Ballin had become what he called a "critical viewer" of the film industry that had developed in New York and in nearby New Jersey in the early and midteens, and virtually all of his criticisms were rooted in the field of scenic design. Along with an overview of his painting career to date and his study in Rome, this was often the focus of his lectures. "Without its setting," Ballin wrote, "a picture production is hopelessly lost, and in more than one instance an otherwise good play has been spoiled by overloaded, overbalanced, or underwrought scenery. There is no greater mission for the art director than to concoct a picture that bears the semblance of composite truth. Motion pictures must tell the truth to be convincing. Beauty affects us by association." He also espoused the view that every emotion can be expressed through form and color, and that "all traits of character can be convincingly suggested by the physical surroundings of the people who are required to feel them."

What particularly intrigued Gibbons was the way in which the older artist had fused two of his own primary interests: architecture and painting, primarily the utilization and composition of space within a frame. In 1912, the year Gibbons began his studies at the League, Ballin received what would turn out to be one of the most important commissions of his career, an assignment to create a series of murals for the newly built Wisconsin State Capitol Building, designed by the architect George B. Post. Ballin's murals illustrated events from the state's history on the curved walls of the building's rotunda, exploding with color and transmuted through the filter of Greek mythology. Critic and poet laureate Louis Untermeyer extolled its virtues in the pages of *Art and Progress* magazine with a stunning bit of divination:

> Altogether this room will be one of the most striking things in America; it will rank with the very finest imaginative thought we have produced, and in sheer force of color will surpass them all. These paintings are both a justification and a prophecy of Mr. Ballin as a decorator!

Not long after Ballin completed the murals, he accepted an offer from the Thomas Edison Studios to work as a set designer and "artistic consultant," but he continued to lecture intermittently at the Art Students League. After one of Ballin's lectures, Gibbons asked George Bridgman for an introduction, and he confidently approached the older artist with a voluminous number of questions about scenic design. Flattered and impressed by Gibbons's astute observations and intelligent queries, Ballin would remember the young Gibbons several years later. In the meantime, Gibbons needed to support himself. His first position after the Art Students League was at Merchants National Bank in New York. In a letter to a former colleague, written two decades later, Gibbons joked that this was where he had begun his "nefarious career." The work bored him, however, and Gibbons left after a few months when he obtained employment as an artist at the J. Walter Thompson Advertising Agency.

In many ways this position, which on the surface might appear to be a departure from the realization of his artistic goals, would in retrospect prove to be a major stepping-stone in Gibbons's career. The decision was also a testament to his pragmatic nature. A steady job in a newly created division of a prestigious ad agency offered security, if not the job of his dreams and the fulfillment of his ambition. He was one of many new employees at the company that year, as the agency welcomed a new president who had recently begun a major restructuring operation, closing branch offices outside of New York as well as expanding, and even creating, entirely new departments.

The J. Walter Thompson Advertising Agency had its beginnings in 1864, when a man named William James Carlton started selling advertising space in small religious magazines. In 1868, twenty-one-year-old James Walter Thompson, after serving in the navy toward the end of the Civil War, joined the two-room operation as a bookkeeper. In his book *Adland: A Global History of Advertising*, author Mark Tungate describes Thompson as "[striding] down a gangplank in New York, determined to carve out a career in the big city." Ten years after going to work for William Carlton, he did so, buying the agency outright for $1,300 ($500 for the company and $800 for the furniture) and giving it his own name.

While working for Carlton, Thompson noticed that while popular magazines stayed in the family home much longer than newspapers, at the time they carried scarcely any advertising. He began to specialize in magazine advertising, and soon the agency became a "full service" firm, pitching advertising slogans to prospective clients, designing the advertisements themselves, and even placing the ads. In 1916, with his health failing, Thompson passed the reins of the company over to the man who would, unwittingly, prove to be yet another mentor to Cedric Gibbons: Stanley Resor.

Thompson had hired Resor to open a Cincinnati branch of the agency in 1908 after hiring him away from Procter & Gamble's in-house ad agency, where he had become well known for his drive and his willingness to innovate. In a rapid expansion of the art and copywriting departments in its New York office, Cedric Gibbons was one of many young artists recruited by the company, undergoing a rigorous and original training program designed to acquaint new employees with what Resor called one of his favorite "scientific" devices: the "Thompson T-Square." It consisted of five questions that Resor felt must be addressed before a marketing plan and advertising campaign could be planned and executed for a prospective client. They were similar to the "who, what, where, when, and why" journalism code that was developed by the Society of Professional Journalists in 1909 and were implemented to gather factual information about a brand name and its competitors.

But if Cedric Gibbons took anything away from his experience at J. Walter Thompson, it was the style and manner utilized by Stanley Resor as he presided over his domain. In appearance, according to Stanley Fox in *The Mirror Makers*, Resor had "more than a touch of the aristocrat." No one ever questioned his authority, although he seldom raised his voice. At the same time, he consciously resisted meddling in the day-to-day work of the agency. His door was always open, and he assumed that people would come to him if there was a problem. It was a method that worked, and would continue to work, once Cedric Gibbons began to organize the fledgling MGM art department in 1926.

A year after Gibbons had been hired at Thompson, he heard from Hugo Ballin, who invited Gibbons to join him at Edison Studios, where he would work as a set dresser and Ballin's assistant. It was in this position that Gibbons would begin to advocate for the use of solid walls and furniture, rather than mere backdrops, in Edison films. Not long after Gibbons joined the studio, Hugo Ballin was presented with his own exciting new opportunity. His reputation as an artist, as well as his writings and lectures on scenic design in motion pictures, had paved the way for a phone call from film producer Samuel Goldwyn's office. Ballin was offered a five-year contract as an art director at Goldwyn Pictures.

Today Goldwyn Pictures, if remembered at all, is seen as either a minor footnote in the stellar career of Samuel Goldwyn, who later became a prominent independent producer, or as an ill-fated predecessor of Metro-Goldwyn-Mayer, which was incorporated when Goldwyn merged with Metro Pictures and Louis B. Mayer Productions in 1924. But years before this, Goldwyn had already established a precedent for highly crafted, "artistic" productions and a belief in the star system that was later amplified at MGM. Indeed, many of the productions that immediately lent the new company its popular and critical cachet—among them Erich von Stroheim's *Greed* and *The Merry Widow*, along with the epic *Ben-Hur*—had actually gone into preproduction under Goldwyn's aegis. From its inception in 1916, the features produced by Goldwyn Studios were promoted in national magazine ads that trumpeted the "Goldwyn Quality." After hiring Hugo Ballin, another publicity campaign was begun, this one focusing on the improvement of the set designs in Goldwyn films.

Ballin's first film for Goldwyn was a genial matrimonial farce based on a play by Edgar Selwyn that had opened on Broadway in 1912. *Nearly Married* was set in a New Jersey roadside inn, and its environs and did not offer Ballin the challenge he was seeking. His next assignment, a World War I drama starring Mae Marsh, called for the construction of a barracks and an army encampment, and he remembered Gibbons's experience as a builder. His timing was fortuitous. In 1918 Cedric Gibbons left his job at Edison to accept a position as Hugo Ballin's assistant at the Goldwyn Studios in New York.

And so the stage was set. Once Gibbons embarked on his new venture, one that would eventually give him the kind of career he had sought for years, he must have found that the celebrity that attended his ascension a decade later needed a more impressive and fitting backstory. As he began a working relationship with Hugo Ballin, it is tempting to wonder if some elements of his mentor's biography, without going into specific details, eventually found their way into his own life history as retold by MGM publicity. The private tutor and trips to Europe that Cedric recalled have their echoes in the actual facts of Ballin's life: studying with portrait painter James Eaton from the age of seven, traveling throughout Europe, and studying in Rome. The "enthusiasm for reform" regarding set design that *Collier's* mentioned in 1933 also echoes Ballin. Fiction mixed with fact very freely in Gibbons's account of his formative years; it seems to parallel the very film sets he spent his life constructing—couched in the illusion of truth. Cedric may not have been expert at executing bends, curves, and arcs on the dance floor at Slapsy Maxie's, but he proved adept at bending the truth, forging himself a slightly new identity to complement his new responsibilities.

Some of these same curves and arcs attended Cedric's decision to maintain that both his father and grandfather were architects, going so far as to suggest that Patrick Gibbons had made contributions to the final blueprint of St. Patrick's Cathedral. Throughout his long career Gibbons would hire a number of architects to work in the art department at MGM, many with prestigious degrees from institutions such as Princeton and Stanford. Especially during the 1930s, in the depths of the Depression, this was often the only kind of work many architects could find. Was he afraid the men he hired would lack respect for him if they discovered he did not actually hold a degree in architecture? By claiming a pedigreed lineage, he did his best to circumvent any such reaction.

But Gibbons's selective embellishments ultimately did him a disservice. His achievements at both Goldwyn and MGM would be impressive enough for a trained architect. For a young man who was homeschooled and never received architectural training on the university level, however, they were extraordinary. And one can't help but speculate what must have gone through Gibbons's mind when he worked with art director William Ferrari to re-create Penn Station for Vincente Minnelli's *The Clock* in 1945. Did he use any of the sketches he had made thirty years before to help bring the set to life? The station could not be reproduced in exact detail for the parameters of a film set, and how it was to be used in a film imposed restrictions on exactly what was reproduced. But Gibbons must have felt, in some sense, that he had come full circle as he watched workmen constructing pilasters of plaster all around him.

In 1918 Gibbons's life and professional experience placed him in a unique and, even more important, receptive situation. With just enough informal training in both drafting and architectural principles along with formal schooling in composition, unity, balance, and the other aesthetics associated with creating a work of art in a variety of visual media, Gibbons was at the same time not yet indoctrinated into any particular movement or style. He had a keen intellect joined with an insatiable desire for knowledge and an equally avid ambition. These attributes, now combined with the fact that he was assisting one of the most renowned artists of his time—one who was determined to make his mark in scenic design for the movies—allowed him to explore, learn, and reflect on what was still a developing art form. Like the Jewish moguls who had begun arriving in California throughout the teens and who would eventually create one of the biggest entertainment empires in history, Gibbons would soon move forward in his chosen profession. Within six years, to borrow a phrase from author Neal Gabler, he would begin to create an empire of his own.

Photo by J.H.Ramsey
Dingman Studio
L.A.

CHAPTER TWO

WANTED: INTERIOR DESIGNERS FOR THE SCREEN

O N MARCH 9, 1907, THE FIRST MOTION PICTURE trade magazine in the United States, *The Moving Picture World*, commenced publication in a cramped office space on lower Broadway in New York City. The journal's founder, J. P. Chalmers Jr., was already the editor of a magazine devoted to still photography, and in an editorial on the first page of his new venture he offered this mission statement: "It is our intention to give the best, and only the best, news concerning the film industry, describing briefly each new film as it is produced, taking note of its quality, and giving an unbiased opinion of its merits or demerits."

Today, leafing through the first issues of *Moving Picture World*, one can't help but get caught up in the entrepreneurial excitement—in reviews, news articles, and advertisements—that almost leaps off each page. "The Motiograph! The projector that prevents tired eyes and headaches!" was available from the Chicago Projecting Company for enterprising nickelodeon owners, but it faced stiff competition from the Edison Kinetoscope, now with "a much larger lamp house than other types of projectors." The Olympic Projectionist School in Manhattan offered hands-on training for people interested in becoming film projectionists, "a job with a future."

While reviews of each week's releases were anonymous and unsigned, they almost invariably touched on and, in some cases, focused on one element: the settings. "The subject is exceptionally well-rendered in the settings and costumes," read the first sentence in a review of *A Poor Knight and the Duke's Daughter*, released by Gaumont in 1908. Essanay Studios, based in Chicago, was frequently cited by the magazine throughout 1908 and 1909 for "the care devoted to the settings" in its pictures.

Yet most of the settings in the earliest silent films were composed of a series of nondescript, characterless flats, sometimes embellished with painted props—large urns with plants, for example, or a table seen in proper perspective. Actual objects were rare. These shortcomings were most evident in films set in a contemporary milieu. As William K. Everson points out in his seminal book *American Silent Film*, "the eventual function of the art director in the early films was usually shared by the director and his cameramen . . . and the best of such teams were often more creative in what they suggested—a cunning arrangement of people and props within the frame, implying an extension of on-screen 'sets' or activity into off-screen space—than in what they actually showed." Chief among these collaborations was the professional relationship between D. W. Griffith and his cameraman Billy Bitzer, who, between 1908 and 1909, worked miracles at the old Biograph studios on Fourteenth Street in New York City, a space that had room for only one set at a time. In the midteens, as Griffith branched out into feature-length

The 1914 Italian production *Cabiria* pioneered an architectural approach to set design, utilizing wood, plaster, and fiber to re-create the buildings of ancient Rome.

filmmaking, concentrating on historical and biblical subject matter, he worked with collaborators such as architect Walter Hall and contractor Frank "Huck" Wortman to create the prodigious sets for *Judith of Bethulia* (1914) and *Intolerance* (1916). An architectural approach to set design had been pioneered in the 1914 Italian production *Cabiria*, with walls and platforms built of wood and glazed with a mixture of plaster and fiber to resemble the stone buildings of ancient Rome. When the film proved to be an international sensation, Griffith was determined not to be left behind. In some ways, *Intolerance* was not just Griffith's answer to those who—in his mind at least—had unjustly accused him of racism after the release of *Birth of a Nation* but also an American retort to Giovanni Pastrone's Italian extravaganza.

Yet the pursuit to find a balance between actual, realistic modern settings and their depiction on the screen was still an ongoing quest, and the editors at *Moving Picture World* provided a platform for critics and commentators to discuss the topic during the early days of film. Louis Reeves Harrison was a leading editorial columnist for the magazine in its first years of publication, covering and interpreting film production as a commercial product as well as a medium of aesthetic innovation. In the June 11, 1911, issue he wrote an editorial titled simply "Settings," in which he extolled the importance of a proper background:

> Good taste is not confined to the homes of those whose wealth enables them to purchase sure [*sic*] examples of fine art but is exhibited in all sections of the country and forms a part of the national character. It would be an object lesson to the people of other countries and a great pleasure to our own people if home interiors on the studio stage closely followed the best example of those in existence.

Wray Bartlett Physioc, a painter and director who made several films in the late teens and early twenties, followed this up a year later in the same publication with an article begging for "restraint in interior decoration," claiming that in one recent release he had seen a drawing room covered with "arabesque ornament" and figures of nymphs and cherubs that would be more fitting for a chamber of horrors.

A turning point of sorts was reached when Wilfred Buckland, previously a set designer for the legendary stage impresario David Belasco, went to Southern California to design Cecil B. DeMille's *The Squaw Man* in 1914. The Jesse Lasky Studio had purchased all the rights to the Belasco stage properties, with Cecil B. DeMille directing, and Buckland was part of the deal. When he arrived at the "studio," however, what he saw astonished him, for it was merely a ramshackle, open-air barn surrounded by lemon groves at the corner of Vine Street and Selma Avenue in Hollywood. The stage featured a ship's mast with a boom upon which a sail could be hoisted for the purpose of keeping the direct rays of the sun away from the action in front of the camera. Perhaps in an effort to quell Buckland's visible astonishment at the sight before him, one of DeMille's assistants informed him that the ship mast rigging was soon to be "improved" by the installation of muslin sheets that could be drawn across the stage.

Whether protected from sunlight or not, many of the sets were still nondescript and aesthetically unappealing. For the backgrounds in many of the indoor scenes, DeMille had sketched diagrams to indicate where he wanted doors and windows to be placed and a carpenter had duly constructed and painted the flats as indicated. With mounting concern, Buckland realized that any attempt to re-create on film what made Belasco's productions unique on stage—dramatic lighting and the use of strategically placed props and furniture to create perspective—would be doomed to failure. Belasco had written a number of plays for his own theater; *Madame Butterfly* and *The Girl of the Golden West* would later be turned into operas by Giacomo Puccini. To reproduce these and other productions on film in broad daylight would sacrifice almost everything that had made them a success in the theater.

In New York, Belasco and Buckland had developed a working relationship with the Kleigl brothers, John and Anton, both of them electricians who had immigrated from Germany. In 1911, the brothers developed a carbon arc lamp they dubbed the "klieg light" that could be used to isolate performers and scenery on a stage. Technicians working at the Lasky studios remained unconvinced that these lights could be used with film because they thought the use of artificial lighting would be too difficult to control. Buckland realized instinctively that precisely the opposite was true as long as the setting was enclosed, and he placed an order for two klieg lights to be sent from New York. While waiting for

Above: Wilfred Buckland, sitting in the car he purchased shortly after his arrival in Hollywood.

Right: Cecil B. DeMille gestures on the outdoor set of *The Squaw Man.*

their arrival, he argued with DeMille and his codirector, Oscar Apfel, that even if everything seen on the screen were not in sharp focus, larger rooms with real furniture and props would lend to the proceedings an air of reality that would be impossible to obtain with painted flats. DeMille ultimately concurred, and when the klieg lights arrived, Buckland was vindicated. Their use soon spread beyond the Lasky studios, but for years the effects the lights created were referred to by the appellation "Lasky lighting."

Buckland's innovations in the midteens were a decisive moment in the development of Hollywood set design. Years later, in 1921, Kenneth MacGowan, a director who would win an Academy Award for Best Color Short Film in 1934, the first live-action short made in the three-color Technicolor process, applauded Buckland when he recalled seeing DeMille's *Carmen*, with Geraldine Farrar, in 1915: "Here were faces, groups, and interiors lit by a warm glow of light, clear and yet full of the modeling of delicate shadows . . . at one point a touch of back lighting shot across the scene, picked out a curve of throat, a twist of bright hair, or a fold of lace for a glowing, glistening highlight." The key features of the impressionist movement in painting, such as the delineation of light in all its changing qualities, along with the perception of movement and unusual visual angles, had moved from canvas to screen.

Another defining moment occurred in 1915, when *House Beautiful* magazine issued a clarion call for more realistic settings in motion pictures. It was the first time that a national, consumer-oriented publication not affiliated with the film industry had addressed the topic. Founded in 1896 by Eugene Klapp and Herbert S. Stone, *House Beautiful* was conceived as a counter influence to deeply entrenched materialistic social patterns and ostentatious design. Frank Lloyd Wright was an early supporter, and the editorial on set design that appeared in the February 1915 issue noted that "it is with considerable surprise that we follow plays from their outdoor scenes to their interiors, and hideous rooms crowded with grotesque furniture, with sentimental pictures in gingerbread frames, with tawdry curtains and glaring carpets. The wall paper shrieks aloud

Lasky lighting: Geraldine Farrar and Pedro de Cordoba in DeMille's *Carmen*.

[and] . . . one gauges the wealth of a character in the movies by the amount of statuary in his drawing room. And in almost every case, whether the house represented be that of a millionaire or the impoverished hero, bad taste reigns."

Coincidentally or not, the years following the publication of this editorial would witness a transformative revolution in motion picture set design, particularly interior sets, in both their conception and execution. Following in Buckland's footsteps, these changes would be facilitated, for the most part, by a number of men, but two stand out: Ben Carré and Joseph Urban. Yet their ideas would not always go unchallenged by powerful figures within the industry, and the struggles that would ensue over competing ideologies—some of them involving the very nature of film itself—would ultimately shape and codify the American film industry's approach to set design for decades.

While Wilfred Buckland introduced artificial lighting tricks in film settings, it was Ben Carré who pioneered the use of applied painting to complement and improve on the standard procedure already in use with painted flats. Born in Paris in 1883, Carré had painted backdrops for the Opéra de Paris, the Comédie Française, and Covent Garden in London before joining Gaumont Studios in 1906. Founded by engineer-turned-inventor Léon Gaumont in 1895, Gaumont was the first established film company in the world, and when Carré was assigned to work on the visual appearance of its films, he was the first to use colored backdrops instead of backgrounds painted in black and white. Carré soon found himself in total control of the visual style of all Gaumont's films. "In 1910," he said, "when I was with Gaumont in Paris, I introduced color into the sets for the sake of the actors, and we found it relieved the hardness of black and white and was more interesting. Contrast must be carefully done." He also pioneered the use of authentic props: "Properties that require close-ups must be carefully selected. A key of five hundred years ago must be of that period. When were letters sealed? When merely rolled?"

Carré arrived in New York in 1912 to take a temporary job with the Éclair Film Company, which was owned by Cinématographs Éclair in France. When the American division shut down in 1914, Carré began a rewarding collaboration with director Maurice Tourneur while freelancing for other studios. One of his greatest triumphs was the set design for Universal's *The Phantom of the Opera* (1925) that starred Lon Chaney. Since Carré had worked at the Paris Opera House, he knew the building intimately, and he produced twenty-four sketches, later admitting that "some of them came right out of my imagination!" In 1937 Carré became a painter on staff at MGM, where he stayed until he retired in 1965. The invention of a process in 1922 had made it possible to enlarge ordinary

Lon Chaney as the Phantom of the Opera. Ben Carré's set depicts the sewers beneath the Paris Opera House.

photographic plates into fifteen- by twenty-foot reproductions that were sharp and clear, and this soon reduced the need for painted scenery in filmmaking. But the creation of skylines for magical places such as Oz, the illusion of endless doorways following one another as Norma Shearer walks down a long corridor in Versailles as Marie Antoinette, and a light cerulean cloud cover to frame Gene Kelly and Cyd Charisse in *Singin' in the Rain* required matte paintings, which were created for everything cited here by Ben Carré.

Joseph Urban, by contrast, was trained as an architect in the avant-garde ambience of the Vienna Secession, an art movement formed in 1897 by a group of Austrian artists who objected to the prevailing conservatism of the time. He designed sets for both the

Boston and Paris Opera, and from 1918 until his death in 1933, he designed all the sets for the Metropolitan Opera in New York. In 1914 Urban began to design the Ziegfeld Follies, and it was at Ziegfeld's New Amsterdam Theater that newspaper magnate William Randolph Hearst first became familiar with his work. Hearst had become smitten with a photographer's model, Marion Davies, who had made her debut as a Ziegfeld Girl in 1916. He formed Cosmopolitan Productions in 1918 to launch and promote Davies's film career, and two years later he approached Urban, already a star in theatrical circles, to design the sets for Cosmopolitan's films. "For Hearst," wrote Juan Antonio Ramírez in *Architecture for the Screen*, "the conclusion was clear: to be recognized as an exceptional artist, Marion Davies need only appear framed by Urban's sumptuous designs."

One of Urban's first undertakings was to redesign the lighting system that was in use at Cosmopolitan. Like Buckland before him, he insisted that light should come from discreet sources, and not simply washed across the set from on high. In the silent era, when color film was virtually unknown outside of hand-tinted prints, Urban also maintained that moviegoers could be made to "think in color" if the sets had proper backgrounds, with furniture and décor that "belonged" in those backgrounds. In order to achieve this, he created black-and-white "color charts" to test how different colors and textures might appear on black-and-white film, and what colors they might suggest in the eyes of moviegoers. The *New York Times* review of *When Knighthood Was in Flower*, a Marion Davies costume drama released in 1922, would seem, initially, to bear out Hearst's decision to hire Urban:

> You are bound to be impressed with the authenticity of the settings. Surely Joseph Urban, who is responsible for them, has been true as well as magnificent. His scenes are splendid or simple, according to the character they should have, and, while they often impress the eye by their size and finished composition, they never seem present merely to be impressive. They are part of the story and ultimately successful in enriching it.

One of Joseph Urban's highly realistic sets for *When Knighthood Was in Flower*.

Urban's initial interest in film sets was triggered by their architectural aspect and the idea that he would be responsible for the creation of a world on film over which he had total control. But dissension soon developed between Urban and the directors he worked with at Cosmopolitan, for he felt they should defer to his artistic decisions and not the other way around. "I want to make pictures," he stated, "that are moving compositions in the same sense that a great painting is an immobile composition. At any point in a photo-play, a photographic 'still' should reveal people and scenery in perfect artistic coordination." This position echoed a similar sentiment that was communicated to Cecil B. DeMille several years earlier in a letter written by a disgruntled Wilfred Buckland: "I was seeking an opportunity [in coming to Hollywood] to picturize in a more painter-like manner, supplying to motion pictures the same rules which govern the higher art of painting," Buckland wrote. "Had I known I was wanted merely to design sets I would never have joined the company." To achieve his goal, Buckland had increasingly interfered with DeMille's direction, insisting on a role when it came to decisions regarding camera angles and other technical matters. In 1920 DeMille abruptly dismissed him.

The fundamental gauntlet that was tossed as each of these art directors rebelled against the limitations imposed upon them was not just who, precisely, was in control of what appeared on the screen, but what, indeed, constituted a "moving picture"? Was it purely a work of visual art, a series of compositions that moved across a screen, or a story much like a play or novel requiring a director to shape and control the narrative flow? The buildup to a confrontation was already in the air when *Moving Picture World* published a symposium in its July 17, 1917, issue titled "Progress of Art in Pictures." In an article titled "A Plea for the Art World," the poet Vachel Lindsay championed the first point of view, admonishing directors to "talk to the greatest and most accredited artists, take them to your films. They will pick out as the chief beauties things you have thought secondary. They will utterly condemn some lavish mess you thought highly decorative. Consider how to identify their moods with the innermost texture of your work and thought and put in vibrant motion what in the museums is in vibrant rest." In two separate articles, Wilfred Buckland weighed in with the belief that "motion pictures are, or should be, pictorial art, so we cannot disregard the judgment of painters, the makers of real pictures," while director Maurice Tourneur felt that "every actor is a human pigment and he must harmonize with the film creation *as I conceive it* [italics mine]."

The blueprint for the role that the art director would eventually play as the studio system began to emerge in the mid-1920s as a means of production was more or less crafted in an agreement that Cosmopolitan reached with its "very unhappy" art director Joseph Urban in 1920, soon after he began work at the studio. It is preserved among Urban's letters at Columbia University, and states that Urban should not become involved in the development of any motion picture until the concept is fixed in the director's mind. The director was also given "maximum freedom" in "executing the production," which basically meant that while Urban had complete autonomy when carrying out his designs, he could not dictate to the director how to shoot or light them.

There were also, during the summer of 1920, a flurry of articles on set design published by *The American Architect*, a periodical on architecture and building published in the United States during the late nineteenth and early twentieth centuries. The editors at the magazine seemed to have reached a unanimous conclusion in the issue dated July 7, 1920: "Within the past year, the larger and more successful producers have been engaging architects to plan and superintend the building of their sets. The results are so satisfying that the differentiation between stage and cinema design now seems to be clear—the former is one of the decorative and the latter one of the structural arts."

But there would be one last plunge into interior design innovation with the arrival of Hugo Ballin at Goldwyn Studios. "It was something even the legitimate theater hesitated to accept," wrote Kenneth MacGowan in *Motion Picture Classic* about Ballin's work; "[there were] settings with simplicity instead of detail, suggestion instead of elaboration, interpretation instead of ornate confusion." But Ballin, too, like Urban and Buckland, would begin to chafe at the restrictions placed on him. He insisted, for example, on indicating where the camera should be placed through arrows he drew on the floor. Ballin soon left the field of art direction and began to direct pictures for Goldwyn, many featuring his wife, Mabel Ballin. It would remain for his assistant, Cedric Gibbons, to assume the mantle of supervisory art director at Goldwyn, eventually helping to define, and then refine, as *American Architect* put it so succinctly, "that half-way ground between reality and romance, which is the evening playground of so many of us."

CHAPTER THREE

GIBBONS AT GOLDWYN

T HE OFFICIAL ANNOUNCEMENT WAS MADE IN the motion picture trade papers on January 27, 1917: "Goldwyn Pictures Corporation has been founded with the intention of contributing three important elements to its feature films—quality, novelty, and standard of production." The agreement had been signed by Samuel Goldfish in a partnership with the Broadway producers Edgar and Archibald Selwyn on November 19, 1916, and the name of the new company came from a combination of their last names. Samuel would later adopt the name as his own.

Samuel Goldwyn in the early 1920s.

Hugo Ballin, for his part, was thrilled to be a part of the new organization. "I have from the very beginning taken the motion picture as a serious medium for artistic expression," he told *Motion Picture News*. "Here at last was something that promised to become a popular art! Since the days of the minstrels who went about ancient lands chanting the glories of bygone days and heroic exploits, there had been no medium to which the great masses of people had an opportunity to respond."

In addition to Ballin, Goldwyn had also hired portrait painter William Cotton and popular illustrator Everett Shinn to assist with set design and construction. Referred to as "the Dickens of the pen

Hugo Ballin in 1924.

and brush" by writer Vivian Moses, a journalist who covered Hollywood during the silent era, Shinn's humorous drawings had become a staple of many American magazines in the days before the widespread use of photography in newspapers and periodicals. Cotton was a portrait painter who had gained wide recognition after winning the Hallgarten Prize for first place in 1907, awarded by the National Academy of Design. Coincidentally, Hugo Ballin came in second that year.

Shinn's renderings for the sets he designed were impressionistic but suggested every detail in a room or scene, including the figures of characters in correct costume. Cotton's approach was similar. Only Ballin tackled the job as an architect might, preparing a plan drawn to scale, usually omitting furniture, figures, and other details. He preferred to add these later after discussions with the director. Vivian Moses waxed rhapsodic over these developments at Goldwyn in the summer of 1917: "This process, not only of eliminating every unnecessary thing, but of making every physical element in a photoplay, no matter how small or how great, no matter how costly or how cheap, place its shoulder to the wheel and help to roll the story along the main path of its progress is the process of real simplification which three eminent artists have brought to Goldwyn Pictures, and it is a new word in motion picture production."

But Moses was prescient as well: "And it is not without the realm of the possible, in things Goldwyn, that when the artist has become sufficiently proficient in the art of directing to stand alone he will direct—alone." Ballin had in fact made his intentions clear and his ultimate goal explicit when he signed with Goldwyn, insisting on a codirector credit with John Robertson for the 1917 comedy *Baby Mine*, the first film featuring stage actress Madge Kennedy. The film was well received, and reviews singled out Hugo Ballin's contributions without actually naming him: "A revelation of the high art of the screen," wrote the critic for the *Philadelphia Public Ledger*. "But it is [in] the latest methods of photography and lighting and the simple taste of the interiors that I took the most interest. The skill of great artists has produced these results." Its sister publication, the *Evening Ledger*, noted that "the picture has many distinctions in addition to star and story—individuality in settings, and no one to date has built such imposing rooms and halls and 'shot' the results from such effective points."

Ballin soon settled into a routine at Goldwyn; his work on each film began with a conference attended by the director and other department heads. For every scene he made a separate sketch, employing a color scale of photographic values that he invented to control the color value of his sets, a scale very similar to the one Joseph Urban had developed at Cosmopolitan. Directly under Ballin were two buyers who purchased everything

Mae Marsh, on a white steed, leads the circus parade through Everett Shinn's village built on the Fort Lee lot of the Goldwyn Studios.

required for the settings, while Edward Wortham, the Goldwyn stage manager, supervised the work of assistants who built the sets. Ballin was also credited with inventing a "life-saving innovation" to lower the summer temperature beneath the great glass roof of the sound stages in Fort Lee. It involved the construction of ducts at each end of the building that would allow air cooled by iced water and powered by a fifty-horsepower engine, to flow through a network of perforated pipes.

◇

Everett Shinn's first assignment at the studio involved designing the sets for *Polly of the Circus*, a Mae Marsh vehicle about the romance between a circus performer and a small-town minister. Shinn built a village that occupied more than two square city blocks on the Fort Lee lot as well as an immense big top for the circus performances. And not far away from Shinn's village, which was left standing for possible use in future productions, Cedric Gibbons built the barracks and army encampment he had been hired by Ballin to create for another Mae Marsh film, this one a World War I melodrama, *Fields of Honor*. No sooner had Gibbons's work been completed than the reality of the real war intervened with his career aspirations. The United States had entered World War I on April 6, 1917, and Gibbons was drafted, serving in the naval reserve at Pelham Bay, New York. During the time that Gibbons was on leave from the studio, a series of dramatic changes would take place at Goldwyn Pictures that would eventually place his star on the ascendant even quicker than he might have hoped.

By 1918 most of the major film studios that had established centers of production in Fort Lee, New Jersey—among them Metro Pictures, Fox Film Corporation, and Lewis Selznick Productions—had relocated to Hollywood, and Goldwyn was, as one trade publication put it, "the last picture plant of the first magnitude left in the east." In April of that year, Sam Goldfish expressed an interest in acquiring the Balboa Studios in Long Beach, an independent producing concern that had voluntarily turned over its plant to the Los Angeles Wholesalers' Board of Trade for liquidation. But the dissolution of the Triangle Film Corporation that summer provided an even greater opportunity.

The Triangle Studio lot had been built in Culver City, California, in 1915 by Roy and Harry Aitken in partnership with filmmakers D. W. Griffith, Thomas Ince, and Mack Sennett. It covered a forty-acre tract of hills and woodlands. The buildings included six huge production stages, and as one trade journal noted, "The glint of sun on these huge steel and glass production stages can be seen for miles around." Storehouses and wardrobe were housed in separate buildings, and these included a complete portrait studio, editing labs, a garage with room for thirty-five cars, and a steel and concrete vault where costly filmmaking equipment could be stored. All of this became Goldwyn's property in the fall of 1918 in an outright cash transfer that was said at the time to have been the largest of

Cedric Gibbons in his office at the Goldwyn Studios in 1923.

its kind ever recorded in the history of the motion picture industry. By 1919 almost all of Goldwyn's production facilities were relocated from New Jersey to Southern California.

Various improvements were begun as soon as the studio passed into Goldwyn's hands. New stages were erected, and the dressing rooms were extended. A large portable electric plant, the first of its kind to be installed in a motion picture studio, was perhaps the most important addition. When Gibbons was honorably discharged from the armed forces, never having served overseas, he quickly left New York City and made the "great migration" to California to resume his chosen career at the new studio lot. In the summer of 1919, he signed a long-term contract with the studio to continue as Hugo Ballin's assistant. Once again Gibbons's timing was propitious, for that same year, Ballin would abandon art direction in favor of directing his own features. He did not return to the field until 1927, when Gloria Swanson commissioned him to design her film *The Love of Sunya*, made by her own production company and distributed through United Artists.

Everett Shinn left Goldwyn after designing only three films, and William Cotton went back to painting after designing only a handful of films, including *The Spreading Dawn*, with Jane Cowl. This left the field clear for Gibbons, and in 1919, he designed his first film for Goldwyn, a story of "East meets West" titled *The Unwritten Code*. The film afforded him the opportunity to design a number of Japanese interiors, but the design ethos Gibbons had absorbed from Ballin would not be fully employed until his next film, *Earthbound*, released in 1920. Goldwyn's advertising department left no doubt as to the film's importance in its release schedule that year: "One year in production, *Earthbound*, as powerful as its title suggests, is destined without question to go down in photoplay annals as one of the masterful sensations of the screen. A mere descriptive paragraph can in no way acquaint you with the bigness of *Earthbound*. You will judge it when you see it."

A story of moral retribution and redemption, *Earthbound* is the story of a man who kills his friend when he discovers the friend is having an affair with his wife. The murdered man's ghost then takes up residence and attempts to positively influence the lives of those he had ruined. The film critic of the *New York Times* noted that while there had been depictions of ghosts in films before, this was the first he had seen in which one was present for much of the film's duration, "and in which were so illustrated the subtleties of its presence, its growing faint to the vanishing point and strong almost to materialization according to the perception of those on this side of death and the dramatic significance of the action." The film's director, Basil King, made effective use of double exposure to create the ghost on film.

In order to emphasize the exclusivity and uniqueness of its new feature on audiences, Goldwyn discarded the traditional methods of release, and arranged to lease the Playhouse, a legitimate theater in Chicago, and the Astor Theater in New York, where indefinite runs would begin on August 11. At each theater, so gradually as to escape attention in the early scenes, a blue light was thrown about the screen from behind the parted draperies that encircled the proscenium arch in each theater. As the rising action began, culminating with the murder of the protagonist's friend, this dissolved into a dull red glow, growing in intensity as the event built to a climax, and finally bursting into a brilliant crimson at the moment of the murder. Most striking of all the lighting effects, however, occurred in the film itself, when the "earthbound" murder victim is freed of his earthly ties and is seen to walk out of the frame and into space. A white shaft of light is then projected diagonally across the screen. It envelops the figure of the woman with whom he had an affair, kneeling beneath a thirteen-foot bas-relief sculpture of Christ on the cross.

The setting that depicted the cathedral interior was Gibbons's first triumph at Goldwyn, and in fact there were few existing sound stages in Hollywood at the time that could have accommodated a set quite so large. If the set had been constructed outdoors on the lot, the lighting effect that so successfully concluded the film would have been next-to-impossible to achieve. The front door of the cathedral set, up the long aisle to the

The final scene in Basil King's production of *Earthbound*, Gibbons's first major success at Goldwyn.

rear door, covered a distance of 240 feet. The width was nearly ninety feet. The seven-branched candlesticks that dotted the set were ten feet in height. The smaller pillars were thirty and the larger seventy feet high. But more important than the dimension of the set was the stark, clean look of it. In the last shot, Gibbons, as much as the camera, focused the viewer's eyes to the central figure in the drama.

"When the set stands out to such a degree that it ceases to assist the director in the dramatic and hinders the cameraman it might just as well be the interior of any home," Gibbons told a reporter in 1923. Or, perhaps, a cathedral. *Earthbound* was a succès d'estime for Goldwyn as well as a box office bonanza. On September 19, when the film moved from its roadshow engagement at the Astor Theater in Times Square to play concurrently at the Capitol, located about eight blocks north on Broadway at Fiftieth Street, six thousand people stormed the box office between 7:00 p.m. and 7:30 p.m., and police reserves from the Forty-Seventh Street station were rushed to the theater to form the crowds into two lines that stretched for three blocks. The following year, in October 1921, Gibbons signed a long-term contract with Goldwyn Pictures to serve in the position of supervising art director.

Gibbons's new position gave him access to the mighty Goldwyn publicity machine, and interviews as well as articles on his work began to appear in popular and specialized journals. *American Architect* headlined an article on Gibbons in November of that year that featured his work on Goldwyn's *Bunty Pulls the Strings*, a farce adapted from a play that was a major hit in both Great Britain and on Broadway. It was in a small Scottish village. Gibbons and his construction manager, Julian Garnsey, were given complete freedom to lay out a church, a tavern, and approximately ten houses, all built from stone, on land adjacent to the Goldwyn lot. Rose vines were taken from the Goldwyn greenhouse and set against the walls of each cottage, which featured thatched roofs. "Here," wrote Jerome Lachenbruch in the issue dated November 3, "in the motion picture at its best, we may find a sincerity in the spirit of the reproduction, and a verisimilitude with the

Gibbons (right, in white shirt) examines the field adjacent to the Goldwyn lot where the Scottish village for *Bunty Pulls the Strings* will be built.

original that cannot fail to stimulate our architectural interests. We may grant the artifice behind the motion picture; but the architectural artifice has, nevertheless, resulted in a close approach to art." Goldwyn thought so too. The company leased the ground for a year and kept the village standing as an exhibition, selling tickets to the general public. The acreage was eventually purchased, and the set would later appear, redressed, in *The Big Parade* (1925), *Storm at Daybreak* (1933), *The Bishop Misbehaves*, and *The Casino Murder Case* (both 1935).

An interior of one of the cottages in *Bunty Pulls the Strings*.

"It is well-known that the motion picture architect deals with genuine architectural problems, but these are all subordinated to the primary purpose of creating a perfect illusion on the motion picture screen. Consequently, his labor is complicated by such pictorial considerations as light effects, composition, and photographic angles," Gibbons told the *Los Angeles Times* in 1921, when he described his working process to reporter J. A. Jackson. This process fused much of the pioneering work that Buckland and Urban had already done in lighting and composition with his mentor Hugo Ballin's beliefs that

Cedric Gibbons can be seen in the second row, fifth from the left, in this group photo of the Goldwyn Studio department heads.

sets should sustain mood and supply a unifying tone and style. But it also brought to bear Gibbons's own sensibilities on concepts of harmonious composition plus the importance of proper procedure and the delegation of responsibility in the construction of sets. Gibbons had never experienced the kind of success that Ballin, Shinn, and Cotton had achieved as individual artists used to working alone. His temperament was more suited to functioning alongside or with a team of professionals:

> First, after reading the story and deciding upon the type of sets to be made, [the designer] draws a number of sketches. These are carefully

gone over with members of the directorial staff, who study the effectiveness of the architectural composition in connection with the dramatic action to be filmed. Many sketches may be beautiful in themselves but may be impractical as motion picture sets.

When the sketches have been accepted the more mechanical elements of the architect's undertaking begin. From the rough design finished, detailed drawings are made of the various sets, viewed from different angles. Dissimilar elevations, acting platforms for balconies, height and arches and other details are all indicated here for the army of blueprint draftsmen who are the next group to add their labor and knowledge to the work in hand.

With the blueprints finished, some of the architect's most arduous work begins. He is not only in constant consultation with the builder in charge of construction, he is also out on the lot, climbing scaffolds, often directing an apparently unimportant detail or devising some means for one of the construction groups to circumvent an unforeseen, and often believed an insurmountable, difficulty.

Virtually all the films that Gibbons worked on at Goldwyn have been lost, victims of disintegrating nitrate film and a fire in a storage facility on the MGM lot in 1965 that destroyed many prints and negatives. Almost all that remains are stills and plot synopses. But the reviews that remain from the newspapers of the day point to a growing, formative talent. In its review of *A Blind Bargain*, the *Cumberland Evening Times* of Cumberland, Maryland, enthused, "The soap bubble ballet in the ballroom sequence is one of the most magnificent spectacles ever screened. Two hundred barrels of soap were required to make the clouds of bubbles amid which a dozen diaphanously clad beauties pirouette. Cedric Gibbons, Goldwyn's art director, proves his genius for film stagecraft in this gorgeous spectacle." A review of *The Invisible Power* (1921), a drama about the rehabilitation of a thief, brought this assessment in the *Bradford Era*, of Bradford, Pennsylvania: "The settings, designed by Cedric Gibbons, show some new artistic effects never before seen on the screen. Powerful impressions of height and depth are obtained by simple designs of two walls of a cell, or a gate to represent a jail." And while there is room for suspicion that these were prepared reviews, supplied to regional news outlets by the Goldwyn Studios marketing department, they nonetheless point to the fact that the studio believed it had a designer talented enough to deserve this kind of promotion. For Goldwyn, Gibbons would re-create the streets of Nome, Alaska, as they looked during the Gold Rush for *The Spoilers* (1923) and a Russian village for *The Rendezvous* (1924) that was complete in every detail, from the pigs in the yards of the log hut homes to the bale of hay in the crow's nest of the lookout post. Penn Station, showing the runway from the trains, the train dispatcher, and the bulletin board where departures and arrivals were announced, was re-created in 1924 for the film *True as Steel*.

A different approach was required for Alan Crosland's film version of Elinor Glyn's *Three Weeks* (1924), starring Conrad Nagel and Aileen Pringle. Glyn was a British novelist and screenwriter who specialized in "scandalous" romantic fiction. She popularized the concept of the "It" girl as personified by Clara Bow, and her risqué plots (tame by today's standards) were targeted, and marketed, to a female audience. The story line of *Three Weeks* revolves around the queen (Pringle) of the mythical kingdom of Sardalia, who flees to Switzerland in order to escape her husband, the brutal King Constantine II. There she meets Paul Verdayne (Nagel), a young, wealthy English nobleman. The queen is known to Paul only as "the Lady." The two have a passionate affair that lasts for the titular three weeks, after which the queen returns to her husband. Later, Paul discovers the Lady's true identity, but before they can meet again, she is murdered by the king.

For this over-the-top, overly emotional "scandalous" scenario of passion and ardor, Gibbons matched Glyn's florid prose with sets that captured the brio of illicit love without resorting to stylistic overkill: "It is my belief," he said while working on the film, "that public tastes should be played up to. We have been playing down to the public long enough. In the settings for *Three Weeks* I have eliminated all detail in design and have

A ramshackle hut constructed on the lot for the Gold Rush drama *The Spoilers*.

The interior of the hut, built inside stage 7 on the Goldwyn lot.

An interior room of King Constantine's palace in *Three Weeks.*

merely suggested the mood of the setting. We have cluttered up our sets with palms, jardinieres, and brass beds. Ten years ago, the director in designing the interior of a wealthy home thought that he must use every piece of furniture, tapestry and gew gaw that he could possibly crowd in the room so the public would think it was a rich man's home. In *Three Weeks*, I am working entirely in line, color, and composition."

A bedroom in the Swiss hotel where the queen decamps after leaving her abusive husband, Constantine. Aside from its Ruritanian elements, the set illustrates Gibbons's concern for "proper balance within a frame," as his Art Students League professor George Bridgman once noted.

Crew members prepare a setting representing the palace in *Three Weeks*.

As *Three Weeks* went before the cameras, however, the film industry began to feel the effects of a severe economic recession that began not long after World War I, in 1920–21. The federal debt had exploded because of wartime expenditures, and annual consumer price inflation rates had jumped well above 20 percent by the end of the war. At the same time, as publicist and author Terry Ramsaye has noted, "The war for motion picture supremacy had moved on to new battlegrounds. Now, in its next phase, it was becoming an issue of theatre seats, real estate investment, and large scale financial investments." Companies larger than Goldwyn's, such as Paramount, were growing even larger, and smaller companies were beginning to outdo the studio. Goldwyn's penchant for hiring high-priced theatrical talent that was not always worth the investment resulted in a $100,000 loss for the studio in 1919. The death knell for Goldwyn may have been sounded that same year when Adolph Zukor, the head of Paramount, decided to raise the price of film rentals to offset the escalation of his stars' salaries. Many small theater owners protested the move, and Zukor, in response, began buying up theater chains across the country. It soon became clear that the only way to remain a player in the motion picture industry was to combine production with exhibition.

(L to R) Director Alan Crosland, Elinor Glyn, and Gibbons use a device that allows the viewer to see how color translates to black and white on film.

Marcus Loew was a theater magnate who had parlayed an initial investment in a penny arcade at the turn of the century into a growing chain of theaters. The crown jewel of his empire, the Capitol Theater in New York City, with seating for over four thousand, opened in October 1919. Seeking a new manager to control production, Loew was put in touch with a producer who ran his own small film company. Louis B. Mayer did not have the large physical plant that Goldwyn had; he rented most of his equipment. And rather than a stable of stars, he hired actors for individual films. But Loew wasn't looking for property. He already had the Goldwyn lot. He was seeking someone with business acumen. In late 1923 he finalized the deal that ultimately resulted in the formation of Metro-Goldwyn-Mayer in April 1924. Mayer became the head of the new studio, and his chief of production, Irving Thalberg, assumed the same responsibilities at MGM.

Contrary to what has been popularly assumed, Cedric Gibbons did not immediately become the head of the new MGM art department as a result of his employment at Goldwyn. At first, he became just another art director that Mayer and Thalberg elected to retain at their new studio. His first contract, signed in 1924, extended his original Goldwyn contract for a period of eighteen months. Before he could establish his sovereignty, he would have to confront a powerful rival.

CHAPTER FOUR

THE EMERGENCE OF METRO-GOLDWYN-MAYER

NOT EVEN A YEAR HAD PASSED SINCE THE incorporation of MGM than Irving Thalberg was promulgating on how the studio would be run:

Specialization in every phase of production is one of the fundamental principles in our formula of making pictures. I believe that the making of any production should be *supervised* by one individual who is responsible for the whole picture, but today production is too complicated for one man to manage every detail of it. Details that used to be considered unimportant are now of prime importance in the making of a picture; details in costuming, fidelity to atmosphere, everything that goes to make a realistic feature. For that reason, we have specialists at the Metro-Goldwyn-Mayer studio who are experts in their lines. This guarantees that our pictures will be of the highest possible artistic standard.

Irving Grant Thalberg, vice president in charge of production at MGM.

It was just such a philosophy, along with the encouragement of William Randolph Hearst, whose company Cosmopolitan now released its films through MGM, that compelled Louis B. Mayer to hire Romain de Tirtoff in 1925. Born in St. Petersburg in 1892, Tirtoff, who went by the name Erté, moved to Paris when he was barely out of his teens and worked for the couturier Paul Poiret from 1913 to 1914. In 1915, he landed a contract as an illustrator with the Hearst publication *Harper's Bazaar*, which is where Hearst first took notice of him. He hired Erté to design sets and costumes for the 1920 film *The Restless Sex*, starring Marion Davies. By 1925 the designer had become a leading exponent of the art deco style in illustration and had designed both sets and costumes for the Ziegfeld Follies and George White's Scandals on Broadway.

Mayer became fascinated with Erté, and the stylist himself was initially ecstatic to be in California. "Ah! This is the place!" he told the *Los Angeles Herald Examiner* upon arrival. "Hollywoodland! Here we will rest—my search is ended." In order to keep him happy, Mayer arranged for Erté's atelier in Paris to be duplicated on the MGM lot—ivory and black, with an ivory barrel ceiling set off by long, narrow, black beams running along the ceiling two feet parallel. Small cubical black lamps, with black tassels attached, were fixed at the end of each beam. As if to add insult to injury, Mayer asked Cedric Gibbons to build it. He agreed to do it, but years later he told the *Los Angeles Times* that he did so on the condition that "if the nabob departed before his contract was up, he [Gibbons] would inherit the office." And Erté had hardly moved in when the honeymoon abruptly ended.

Erté's first assignment was to design the sets and costumes for the film *Paris*, but there were script problems and the project was delayed. To keep him busy, he was asked to design costumes for other productions, including Tod Browning's *The Mystic* and *Time, the Comedian*. When *Paris* was finally ready to go before the cameras, the realities of the schedule resulted in Erté's resignation. "I came here seven months ago full of illusions about all the wonderful things I could do in motion pictures. But I have been waiting all that time for the story of my first production to be finished. It has been written four times.

Louis B. Mayer, cofounder of Metro-Goldwyn-Mayer studios in 1924.

Romain de Tirtoff (Erté) in his office on the MGM lot in 1925.

Now they tell me they want me to design everything for a new story in three or four weeks. It is impossible."

Erté's last assignment was to create a headdress for Carmel Myers as an Egyptian siren in *Ben-Hur*, the foundering production of General Lew Wallace's bestseller, which was filming in Italy with mounting costs that were causing mounting concern in Culver City. The property had been in preproduction at Goldwyn when Mayer and Thalberg took over the reins at MGM.

As one of several art directors on staff, Gibbons initially had nothing to do with *Ben-Hur*. Horace Jackson, a Los Angeles architect, had been hired to construct the sets and was already in Rome by the spring of 1924. On a plateau outside the city, Jackson and his crew built what was deemed by publicity to be the largest set ever created for a motion picture: a reproduction of Jerusalem's Joppa Gate. It towered 150 feet into the air and was larger than the original. Initially hampered by Italian bureaucracy, the set took months to build, and in retrospect it can be seen as a metaphor for the entire Roman location shoot. Bess Meredyth, who wrote the original scenario for the film, sent the following cable to Mayer in July: "We have some very beautiful sets going up. Funny thing—we saw a picture made here—*Messalina*—and when we saw the size of their sets realized we had to step up our game."

But in striving for the sensational, Thalberg, for one, found that when he viewed footage sent from Italy, "the scope and size of the spectacle was there, but what was happening up front was drab and lifeless." He began to beg Marcus Loew to bring the production back to the studio, but Loew was unmoved. At the end of 1924 Mayer decided to travel to Rome to survey the situation for himself after receiving a telegram from A. S. Aronson, the head of European operations for MGM, in mid-November. "Frankly," Aronson wrote, "I want to say to you that the quicker we leave this country the better it is. It is remarkable that with all the money we have spent, every time that we go into a set we seem to be missing so many things that we must have." When Mayer arrived, he was appalled at all the money that was being wasted. Eventually he managed to convince Loew to abandon the Italian location, and the *Ben-Hur* company returned to California having spent two million dollars. Less than a third of the film had been completed. Grumbled Thalberg, "I could have made the whole thing right here for $800,000."

At Thalberg's request, Gibbons contacted Ferdinand Earle, a man who had been doing matte paintings and other visual effects in Hollywood since 1917. By the end of March, Gibbons had written Thalberg to tell him that Earle had agreed to create the following shots: the Valley of the Lepers, the star of Bethlehem, the flight into Egypt, and four

Above: (Front row, L to R) actress May McAvoy, Gibbons, director Fred Niblo, and Horace Jackson review the architectural plans for the Antioch Colosseum set in *Ben-Hur*. Ramon Novarro (left) and Francis X. Bushman hover above them, surrounded by construction workers who will eventually build the set.

Left: (L to R) Gibbons, Fred Niblo, May McAvoy, unidentified, Ramon Novarro, and Francis X. Bushman review progress on the construction of the set.

Above: The Antioch Colosseum set for *Ben-Hur* in the early stages of its construction.

Right: Plaster and cement are added to the wooden frame to complete the Colosseum set.

separate images of Roman legions. These images would be a combination of miniatures and animated figures in the foreground.

Recalling that the chariot race had thrilled audiences on the stage, Thalberg allocated three hundred thousand dollars to construct a facsimile of the Antioch Colosseum at the intersection of Venice and La Cienega Boulevards in Los Angeles and entrusted Cedric Gibbons with the design. When he saw Gibbons's initial drawings, Thalberg said, "The audience is going to think the set is a fake unless we prove to them it isn't. What we need are some statues, huge statues we can place the extras beside [*sic*] so the audience

An aerial view of the set under construction.

The glass miniature, perched above the actual set. "This is the miracle conceived by Cedric Gibbons and A. Arnold Gillespie," wrote film historian Kevin Brownlow.

will get a sense of the scale." Gibbons agreed, but he added his own touch. Rather than gazing straight ahead, the two towering male figures at each end of the Colosseum were crouched with their heads turned sideways, as if straining to see down the long stretch of track that passed and curled around them. It was a masterstroke, intensifying the drama of the race itself. These plaster titans looked as if they were riveted at each turn, craning their necks to see as the chariots swept past them. Thalberg had German sculptor Eugene Maier-Kreig build the two colossi to be situated at the end of the spina.

In the final film, as the chariot race is about to begin, there are titillating glimpses of the entire set as hordes of extras, representing the citizens of Antioch, file into the stadium. The bottom portions of gargantuan pillars dwarf both the masses that troop past them on foot and the dignitaries that glide by them, hoisted in upholstered litters. Finally, as film historian Kevin Brownlow describes it in *The Parade's Gone By*:

> The sequence fades in on a line of mounted trumpeters, signaling the start of the event; the camera then tracks slowly behind a squadron of cavalry as it leaves the building and enters the arena. The line of horsemen advances through the huge pillars of the amphitheater; the camera emerges with them and draws to a halt. There is a momentary pause. The horsemen continue trotting forward. Then, very slowly, the camera tilts up and reveals what appears to be the biggest set in film history, filled with the largest crowd ever seen on film. This is the miracle conceived by Cedric Gibbons and A. Arnold ("Buddy") Gillespie.

"We had two little hanging miniatures," Gillespie recalled years later, "with little dolls which [*sic*] we worked with poles from under the seats. The dolls got up and cheered whenever the real people below would move." Having designed these miniatures, Gibbons and Gillespie then devised a glass shot, in which part of the background is painted or photographed in miniature on a glass slide and placed in front of the camera to blend with the rest of the image. which would combine with the full-size set. As Brownlow notes, "When the camera photographed the miniature and the full-size stand together, the perspective was destroyed. The model looked as if it were a part of the actual, constructed set. But most extraordinary of all, Gibbons and Gillespie designed the miniatures so that the camera could pan over them, and not lose register. With a glass shot, the camera has to be in a rigid position; a fraction of an inch out of place and the painted top of a building will appear on screen several yards away from the full-size lower half. This design gave the cameraman complete freedom." Add to this the fact that only one side of the structure actually had to be built, for use in medium shots and close-ups, and Gibbons and Gillespie saved MGM at least one hundred thousand dollars.

Director Niblo and his crew prepare for filming. The extras positioned in front of the columns in the background indicate the vast size of the set. One of Gibbons's plaster titans, looking sideways, can be seen at right.

At the end of the chariot race, Ben-Hur, played by Ramon Novarro, rides slowly to the viewing stand to receive his laurel wreath. In a very real way, Gibbons and Gillespie received their own wreaths at the same time. Gillespie, a graduate of Columbia University and the Art Students League, would eventually become head of MGM's special effects department, and Gibbons was tapped to assume the title he had held at Goldwyn: Supervisory Art Director. It was a position that would eventually make him one of the most powerful executives at MGM. For Thalberg's experience with *Ben-Hur* led him to make a crucial decision: Never again would he allow a production to travel abroad, away from his watchful eyes. With very rare exceptions, every film made by MGM—whether the setting was prerevolutionary France or modern midtown Manhattan—would be shot at Culver City. It was now up to Cedric Gibbons to make that happen.

The art department that Gibbons would assemble was partially modeled on the system Thalberg himself had stabilized as head of production at MGM. Thalberg depended on a small circle of producers who worked closely with him to prepare projects for the cameras. Once production began, they would manage the day-to-day progress of each film and address any problems that arose. Thalberg himself would directly supervise the production of a select number of films each year. These would eventually include, among others, *Grand Hotel*, *Mutiny on the Bounty*, *China Seas*, *Camille*, *Romeo and Juliet*, and *The Good Earth*.

Similarly, Gibbons slowly expanded the art department so that it resembled a large architectural office, dividing it into independent yet coordinated units that included a prop department, miniature and special effects departments, and a unit that specialized in process photography, all under his direct supervision. Gibbons created the general ideas, form, and purpose of the setting, and he retained approval of the execution. The actual development and implementation of the work was left to the individual art directors who reported to him. And, like Thalberg, Gibbons would personally design a few select films each year.

By the late 1920s, Gibbons supervised six unit art directors, twenty draftsmen, two sketch artists, and a select number of set dressers who provided each set with furniture and other accessories. In ten years, this number would expand to seventeen unit art directors and eighty draftsmen. An art director usually juggled two productions at a time, and during the late silent period the design process became streamlined. When a script was in the final stages of preparation, it was passed along to Gibbons, who read it and assigned it to an art director. After the script was approved, Gibbons scheduled a meeting

Sketch artists and unit art directors shared office space in this photograph of the Metro-Goldwyn-Mayer art department in the early 1930s.

with the producer, director, screenwriter, sound engineer, cinematographer, and the art director he had assigned to the project. The story was discussed in detail, and the unit art director called in sketch artists to prepare preliminary versions of each set. If necessary, the unit art director might first confer with the research department if a setting belonged to a specific historical period.

When the sketches of each set were finished and the producer had estimated the costs for producing each one, Gibbons called another meeting of the principals involved in the production. Any problems, such as the location of a door or window, or questions about atmospheric detail were reviewed. Gibbons might ask for changes, and once he had approved the sketches, small wooden models of the sets were constructed to scale. These models gave the director and the cinematographer an opportunity to figure out how the actors would move through the sets, and how they would be lit on the sound stage. Draftsmen then began to work on the complete layouts for each set, taking the camera and any photographic possibilities into account. The final cost estimates were made from these plans. During these preliminary weeks, Gibbons also worked with J. J. Cohn, the production manager at MGM, to determine the exact floor space needed for each set so that various sound stages could be requisitioned before the film began. This was a mandatory safeguard to prevent the overlapping of productions. As each set reached completion, the set dressers moved in, and by the next morning the completed set was turned over to the director and filming began.

But while Thalberg has been lauded as a "boy wonder" and a "producer prince," Gibbons came under fire at the end of the studio era, denounced as someone who took credit for the work of other people. While it is undoubtedly true that there were some designers who festered under the system Gibbons devised—Richard Day, for one, who began his career designing for Erich von Stroheim, worked at MGM in the 1920s, and left in 1930 to freelance—there were many others who stayed for decades, among them Preston Ames, Randall Duell, Jack Martin Smith, Edwin B. Willis, William Horning, and Arnold Gillespie. What set Gibbons apart from Thalberg was Gibbons's supposed insistence that his name appear in the credits for every MGM film; Thalberg felt that "credit you give yourself is not worth having." Was it just a matter of ego that separated the two men? Yes and no—for while it is true that Gibbons's name appears in the credits for most MGM films as supervising art director, it does not appear in every single one, and the stipulation that it must appear is not to be found in any of his studio contracts that are housed along with many of his personal papers and correspondence at the Center for Motion Picture Study of the Academy of Motion Picture Arts and Sciences. There were occasions, particularly in the early 1930s, when Gibbons gave an art director carte blanche and did not involve himself with any overt design decisions unless he was called upon to consult. On these admittedly somewhat rare occurrences, only the unit art director received credit. In the opening titles for *The Cat and the Fiddle* (1934), for example, Alexander Toluboff received sole credit for set design, and Merrill Pye was the only art director acknowledged in the titles for Raoul Walsh's *Going Hollywood* (1933), with a separate credit for set decorator Edwin Willis. Fredric Hope and Hobe Erwin received dual credit for *Dinner at Eight*, one of MGM's most prestigious releases in 1933, and Toluboff and Hope shared the credit for the sets in *Riptide*, Norma Shearer's comeback film in 1934 after a two-year absence from the screen.

Edward Carfagno, who began working as an illustrator at MGM in 1933 and became a full-fledged art director after working as an assistant on *Woman of the Year* (1942), remembers that "Gibbons usually had or shared the credit. That was the normal procedure at the time at MGM, at Paramount. . . . If something went wrong and a director complained that a set wasn't what he had been promised, however, it was Mr. Gibbons who would go down and look at it and say, 'Oh, yes, that was what we promised you' or, if it wasn't, he'd admit it and we'd change it. He was a very good person, besides having excellent taste and being a great organizer. He really was a great guy."

"Organization" was another of Gibbons's major responsibilities as a supervisor, one that took up a great deal of his time and is not generally acknowledged in accounts of his career. In a memo dated November 11, 1936, Gibbons lobbied an executive producer at the studio, Alexander Lichtman, for more sound stages. Expressing the opinion that the studio's current space was "woefully inadequate," Gibbons went on to point out that Warner Brothers had 680,000 square feet compared to 306,000 square feet at MGM. Further, Gibbons drew attention to the fact that "an average production of today requires 30% more stage space than it did four years ago." At the time the memo was written, he noted that his job had become extremely complicated due to the fact that 75 percent of available sound stage space was taken up by just five productions.

Gibbons received approval for additional sound stages without a struggle. By 1936 his power at the studio was such that he encountered few obstacles from the front office when he made a request. From the very beginning, when he hired Erté, Mayer was cognizant of the importance of good design and its role in both creating and marketing a film. And Gibbons and his associates at MGM were creating, in the words of Donald Albrecht, "the most valuable design legacy of any Hollywood studio."

CHAPTER FIVE
MGM MODERNE

IN THEIR BOOK *ART DECO: 1910–1939*, ARCHITEC-
ture historians and curators Charlotte and Tim Benton et al.
wrote that "part of the fascination of the style lies precisely
in its confrontation of new values with old." And this confrontation
is precisely what Cedric Gibbons and Richard Day planned to
create when they conceived the art deco sets for the film *Our
Dancing Daughters* in 1928. It was MGM's first overt attempt
to use an art deco setting in order to underscore and support
a narrative. The film was based on a serial, "The Dancing Girl,"
that had appeared in William Randolph Hearst's *Cosmopolitan*
magazine. Hearst immediately bought the film rights for his
Cosmopolitan Productions and the author, Josephine Lovett,
adapted her story into a screenplay.

A sense of the "new" and "up-to-date" permeated the advance publicity for *Our Dancing Daughters*. It was the first film with sound effects to play the Capitol Theater in New York and the first film at MGM to be made using the new incandescent lighting that would soon become an industry standard. The Hearst press, with its nationwide network, began to promote the film months before its release, and innovation and freshness was the theme. "The new lights work many reversals of color effects in films. Joan Crawford's flaming red hair, under the old lights, would take as black," reported the *New York News* in March. And that's not all the new lights did, according to the *New York Review*:

> Bad colds and similar complaints will not be any excuse for motion picture players hereafter for the newly perfected incandescent lights, it has been discovered, hold therapeutic powers that render them an invaluable curative agency. Dr. Harry Anderson, resident physician at the MGM studio, where the new lights are being used exclusively in a new production, made the discovery last week. Dorothy Sebastian, playing a lead role in *Our Dancing Daughters*, was unwilling to hold up the production because of a severe cold and summoned the physician to the set for advice. "Rest yourself under these lights in between scenes," he ordered. "They have the same light rays that have proven so beneficial in medical treatments."

These incandescent lights led to the development of what came to be known in the 1930s as the "great white set." It was a creation born of lighting techniques as much as décor, in particular high key lighting that created a silken, shiny gleam with few shadows to obscure walls, floors, and furnishings. Beginning late in 1929 Gibbons and his staff would begin consulting with the cinematographer on each film, discussing—and sometimes debating—on how individual sets should be lit. Any close-ups of the stars, of course, were left to the discretion of the cameraman, the individual actors, and the director. The use of key lighting would become a trademark and a brand for many MGM films in the early sound period. It would be copied by Busby Berkeley and also by RKO for their Astaire/Rogers musicals.

The majority of the attendant publicity for *Our Dancing Daughters*, however, concerned the sets. The *Orlando Evening Star* was quite succinct in a feature article: "The sets are ultra-modernistic, typifying the very latest in the French school of modern interior decoration. Such sets are considered the only proper background for this story of hectic youth." An article in the *New York News* was written so far in advance of the film's release that it referred to the movie's working title: "Modernistic effects in furniture and architecture are being used with a vengeance by MGM in *The Dancing Girl*, Joan Crawford's new picture. Weird beds, almost to the floor, have little wood work frame save foot-high boards which conceal the springs and do away with the conventional legs of a bed. These are set against a wall whose only ornamenting [*sic*] is the shape of the doors. Black statues set against gold papered panels form the only ornamental note. The whole thing is being photographed under the new huge incandescent lights."

When the film was released that fall, the *Los Angeles Times* summed up the prevailing reaction: "If you are looking for snappy, up-to-the-minute entertainment in people, sets, and atmosphere it's it and that's that." What nearly every review of the time failed to mention, however, is that only one set in the film was "up-to-the-minute," and the almost startling contrast between the art deco–inspired sets and the other settings provides at least part of the film's narrative thrust.

Our Dancing Daughters tells the story of three young socialites and their fluctuating relationships with friends, parents, and potential boyfriends. Diana Medford (Joan Crawford) has a flashy, colorful personality that has earned her the nickname "Dangerous Diana," yet this moniker conceals a thoughtful and considerate nature. Beatrice (Dorothy Sebastian) is kept on a short leash by her strict parents but she has already "strayed" and is afraid to tell her boyfriend about certain events in her past. Ann (Anita Page) is

The art deco home of "dangerous" Diana Medford (Joan Crawford) created a sensation when *Our Dancing Daughters* was released in 1928.

outwardly sweet and innocent but coldly calculating on the inside, goaded by an equally devious and manipulative mother.

Each daughter in the film is introduced in her home environment, and Diana is the one who lives with her parents in an ultramodern setting. It is as bold as her personality: highly stylized, showcasing geometric patterns with hard angles and curvilinear archways, nude walls, and black terrazzo floors devoid of rugs and carpeting. And not

Above: In stark contrast to Diana's "up-to-the-minute" home, Beatrice (Dorothy Sebastian) and her brother Freddie (Edward Nugent) live amid Edwardian furnishings that reflect the straitlaced and old-fashioned moral point of view of their parents.

Left: Ann (Anita Page) and her mother live in an apartment hotel that suggests transience and limited funds. Ann's mother is determined to have her daughter marry into money.

Director Harry Beaumont (seated) speaks with Edward Nugent before filming commences on an art deco set in *Our Dancing Daughters*.

insignificantly, it is flooded with light, as if symbolically accentuating the fact that Diana has nothing to hide from her mother and father. "If I do say it," she says, "I picked myself some snappy parents!" Her home stands in stark contrast to the residence where Beatrice lives, shrouded with heavy curtains and Edwardian furniture, or the setting Ann inhabits with her mother, an apartment with sparse and desultory furnishings and the suggestion that her mother is either divorced or widowed. When Ann and Diana both vie for the attentions of a young millionaire, Ann's deceptive nature is initially triumphant until her true character is revealed. If *Our Dancing Daughters* can be said to have a theme, it might read something like this: "Don't mistake a girl's frankness and gayety for careless morals."

The film became a manifesto, and its overwhelming success took MGM by surprise. When *Our Dancing Daughters* had its premiere in New York, the lines in front of the Capitol Theater on Broadway stretched for blocks. Disregarding fire regulations, people stood five deep behind the last row of seats in an auditorium that accommodated 5,300 people. Emboldened, Cedric Gibbons began experimenting with art deco décor in a number of films during the late silent period. Many of these sets were featured in films starring Greta Garbo, whose image in the late 1920s had evolved into a smart, willful, "modern" young woman, a fair distance from the early temptresses she had played when she first arrived at MGM in 1925.

A Woman of Affairs was based on Michael Arlen's scandalous bestseller *The Green Hat*, and as the first title informs the audience, it is "the story of a gallant lady—a lady who was perhaps foolish and reckless beyond need—but withal a very gallant lady." In Arlen's novel, the gallant lady was named Iris, but in the film, Garbo is Diana Merrick—another "dangerous" Diana. Risking censure and denunciation, she sacrifices her own reputation to protect those she loves, and she lives surrounded by the same style of art deco furnishings that made their first appearance in *Our Dancing Daughters*.

The art deco home where Diana Merrick (Greta Garbo) lives with her brother Jeffry (Douglas Fairbanks Jr.) in *A Woman of Affairs*.

In contrast to the Merrick home, Neville Holderness (John Gilbert) lives with his father Morton (Hobart Bosworth) in a traditional setting. It is well-established in the film that Morton disapproves of the Merricks and their lifestyle.

As Arden Stuart in *The Single Standard* (1929), Garbo is a feminist ahead of her time, juggling numerous suitors and believing that only one "standard" should exist for both men and women. When we first see her, Arden is standing on the terrace of a house that resembles a geometric cube. It is embellished with recesses along one wall. Two topiaries guard the entrance, growing in a pair of huge stone tubs that are embraced on their sides by art deco frieze work. "Let's go for a drive," she tells her chauffeur, leaning against a stone balustrade and wrapping her arms around his shoulders. "I feel like doing seventy!" Keenly aware of her allure in *The Kiss* (1929, and the last silent made at MGM), Garbo applies makeup in her art deco boudoir and proclaims at the end of the film, when

The ivory and white, almost chaste, hospital where Diana is admitted after she suffers a nervous breakdown.

In *The Single Standard*, Garbo (here with John Mack Brown) plays a feminist ahead of her time, and her surroundings complement her modern outlook.

on trial for the murder of her husband (in order to save the life of a young man, played by Lew Ayres), "I have always been a faithful wife, and I have nothing to reproach myself with. I am indifferent to public opinion!"

The apotheosis of pure art deco design at MGM was reached late in 1929 with a sequel to *Our Dancing Daughters*. *Our Modern Maidens*, released almost prophetically a month before the stock market crash in October, was a sequel only in the sense that it depicted "jazz mad youth." Dorothy Sebastian is missing from the cast, while Joan Crawford and Anita Page play completely different characters. As Billie Brown, the daughter of an automobile tycoon, Crawford lives in a house so theatrical and sensational that it ultimately belies almost every notion its designer—abetted by unit art director Merrill Pye—had ever publicly stated about the purpose and function of successful set design.

Just as haute couture can be a showcase for a designer's most outrageous and innovative ideas, as well as a statement of technical ability, many of the sets for *Our Modern Maidens* take the distinguishing characteristics of art deco interior design and inflate them to almost outlandish proportions. The difference is that, unlike a gown that is not

A parlor in *The Kiss* once again reveals Gibbons's penchant for composition within a frame.

Greta Garbo's art deco boudoir in *The Kiss*.

pragmatic for everyday wear and usually intended only for the runway or for exhibition purposes, the sets for *Our Modern Maidens* were still expected to serve a practical function. "A set," Gibbons wrote in the early 1930s, "can of itself tell a whole story. To design it, one must study the characters in the play, and try to personify them in their settings. Then one must examine the dramatic action and see that no detail in the set might catch the eye and detract from the story. The ideal setting so perfectly blends itself with the action of the drama that one enhances the other. In short, a movie set should never talk. That should be left to the cast." But many of the sets for *Our Modern Maidens* drown out the cast and then essentially obliterate them within their cavernous dimensions and overwhelming décor. The living room of the Brown residence, which took up an entire sound stage, features a massive semicircular entrance edged with molding in a sawtooth design that suggests the folds of an accordion. A curving, multifaceted staircase coils around the fireplace in the middle of the room and leads to a balcony that overlooks the vast living space. The star herself had reservations, as she told a reporter:

> "Really, the architecture is splendid, and it just reeks of jazziness and gayety, but everything is so spacious and there is entirely too much room to make it a cozy home," said Joan Crawford as she gazed at the gorgeous ballroom set which comprised the living room of her newest picture home. "After all, the novelty soon wears off, and the impressiveness of the futuristic design becomes too pronounced. Just for a change I love the rather crossword puzzle effect which is so overpowering when one first beholds it, but for a nice quiet home I prefer the old-fashioned comforts of years ago. Why, look at that archway. Those edges remind me of a buzz saw, and those windows look just like spider webs. And the floors, with their black, silver, and gold black paintings resemble a camouflaged battleship . . . it just wouldn't do as a daily livable atmosphere."

The design strategy for Crawford's bedroom in the film was an even more pronounced, if less showy, example of deco interior design taken to the edge of the extreme. She sleeps in a glass-trimmed bed, overlooking perhaps a dozen glass images of dogs, dolls, and other knickknacks. Flowers in the room are all blown-glass, and wall trimmings, doorknobs, tabletops, telephone equipment, and even sections of the fireplace are constructed of the same breakable material.

Above: (L to R) Joan Crawford, Douglas Fairbanks Jr., and Anita Page dwarfed and virtually engulfed by Gibbons's ostentatious set.

Right: Anita Page and Douglas Fairbanks Jr. in *Our Modern Maidens.* Gibbons's assertion that no set should ever "catch the eye" and overshadow the narrative went out the window with this film.

Gibbons himself later acknowledged, in the most roundabout way possible, that the designs for *Our Modern Maidens* may have detracted from, rather than supported, the dramatic action of the film:

> The settings of major productions of the past few years have undoubtedly reached their climax in spectacle, detail, and cost. It is practically impossible to go further, and what's more it is unnecessary. Now is the time to effect a more dramatic and simple background. This may be accomplished by a greater understanding of dramatic values on the art of the set designer.
>
> In the past the designer of settings has built a probable background for the action of the story. Now he must go one step further; he must design dramatic background of corresponding value to the theme of the picture. By that I mean a background that augments the drama transpiring before it. The key note of this is making the set act with the players.
>
> For instance, if a stairway set is required with action on the steps, the only essentials are the actors, the stairs, and the lights. All else should be subordinated so that we may see the actor as easily as possible and not have our eyes confused with useless and unnecessary detail. For often because of this mass of costly detail some settings seem to be a puzzle, the problem being to find the actor.

The decadence of the sets in *Our Modern Maidens*, in retrospect, seem like an extravagant "last hurrah" for the jazz age. It wasn't until 1932 that most of the American film studios began to really feel the economic pinch of the Crash. MGM was actually the only studio in Hollywood to remain profitable that year; nevertheless Louis B. Mayer sent out a request to all employees to take a salary cut that summer, and the letter he sent to Gibbons has been preserved among his papers: "We extend to you our appreciation of your fine spirit and the evidence of your devotion to our firm in your acceptance of the reduction in salary commencing July 21, 1932, which reduction we hope will be very temporary and will be discontinued as soon as conditions in the theater business improve. This reduction is necessary because of conditions being as bad as they are and because of the possibility of their becoming even worse. In no other way is your contract affected and we look forward with great anticipation to the time when we can resume payment of the full compensation provided for under your contract."

The publication of the Payne Fund Studies in 1934 added to the film industry's woes. This was a five-year research program that had surveyed the effects of Hollywood films on young people, concluding that they had led to a decline in moral values. Films such as *Our Modern Maidens* (where Anita Page's character becomes pregnant as the result of an affair) and *The Kiss* (in which Garbo literally gets away with murder) were inextricably tied to their art deco interiors. The stock market crash of 1929 had accelerated the popularity of what has come to be known as streamlined moderne; in Europe it was more often called art moderne. As Anne Massey has noted, "Use of the moderne style [was seen] as a more acceptable alternative to the morally 'corrupt' art deco style." The magazine *Upholsterer and Interior Decorator*, in an article titled "Who Are These People?" noted that "some time ago, there emanated from the office of Will Hays the suggestion that along with the Board of Censors to protect the public against the influence of moral turpitude, there should be a Board of Art Censors to protect the public against the insidious influence of movie decorators. We hardly think the public needs this protection." Apparently too many undraped art deco statues had found their way onto too many sets. Nothing came of the suggestion.

Art moderne was characterized by simple aerodynamic curves that replaced and softened the jagged edges and sharp angles of the art deco style. It became more or less a celebration of the machine age, with artificial materials such as concrete, metal, and Bakelite, a synthetic plastic, replacing stone and wood. While ornamental and decorative features retained much of the stylized, geometric shapes of art deco, they were smoother and less startling.

Gibbons embraced the new style as early as 1930, and as curator and architectural historian Donald Albrecht has noted, "Under Gibbons' leadership, MGM's sets were the premier showpieces of 1930s films, its designer versatile enough to work in a broad range of contexts, extending from the hard-edged luxury of penthouses for Garbo to the comfortable warmth of the *Thin Man* home."

In the early 1930s, however, the economic realities of the Depression changed the way moderne and deco-influenced sets were used and perceived in films at MGM. In *The Easiest Way* (1931), working girl Laura (Constance Bennett) accepts the invitation of her boss, wealthy Will Brockton (Adolphe Menjou), to move in with him. After falling in love with a young newspaperman, Jack Madison (Robert Montgomery), she leaves Brockton to wait for Madison's return from a job in South America. Soon running out of money, she goes back to Brockton and then Jack suddenly reappears. The film addresses the new reality of life in the wake of the Depression—working girls struggling to make ends meet—but the other side of this reality in these early sound films is the fact that what was once referred to as "up to the minute" design is now offered up as, ultimately, an object of scorn. "Do you like this place?" Brockton asks Laura when she arrives at his penthouse. "Oh, every time I come here, I feel like someone else, like a girl in a storybook or a play. It's wonderful feeling." But when Laura falls for Jack, she tells a friend, "I wouldn't mind being poor with him." Love trumps interior design.

For *Susan Lenox, Her Fall and Rise* (1931), Alexander Toluboff, who worked on the settings with Gibbons, explained how the backgrounds were meant to achieve a visual synchronization with the events of the drama. Born illegitimate and raised in an abusive home, Susan (Greta Garbo), née Helga, flees from her cruel, devious uncle and an arranged marriage and falls in love with Rodney (Clark Gable), a kindhearted stranger. When circumstances force her to run off again, she becomes a woman of easy virtue in order to survive. Regarding the home that Susan flees, Toluboff explained, "There was not a single timber in this setting that was not out of plumb [not exactly vertical]. We

Above: The entryway
and terrace in Brockton's
apartment.

Right: Laura (Constance
Bennett) and Brockton
enjoy breakfast in
the dining nook.

Above: William Brockton's (Adolphe Menjou) art moderne office in *The Easiest Way*.

Left: Laura's home before she moves into William Brockton's penthouse is a tenement flat that she shares with her parents and several siblings. This kitchen set from *The Easiest Way* is evidence that MGM's art directors were quite capable of creating stark realism when it was necessary.

sought to make it as ugly as possible, so uninviting that you immediately understood the plight of this girl." The lighting in these sequences, borrowing heavily from German expressionism, helped to achieve this goal. When the setting moves to Gable's mountain lodge, where Susan takes refuge after running away, Toluboff said, "We made everything as attractive as possible to contrast this dramatically. A huge fireplace made it at once warm and cheery. The rustic decorations and appointments were cozy and inviting. When you see the girl enter, you know it looks like heaven to her after what she has been through. The New York penthouse [where Susan lives as a "kept woman" toward the end

Cinematographer William Daniels accentuated the abusive home Susan shared with her uncle by lighting the set in a style that was redolent of German expressionism.

Rodney's rustic lodge in *Susan Lenox* provides Susan with a safe haven away from her devious uncle.

of the film], beautiful as it is, is cold and mocks the sacrifice she must have made. It has a label of shame stamped upon its gorgeousness."

Whether or not the penthouse had a "label of shame" is a moot point. However, the disparities between the art deco home in *Our Dancing Daughters* and the apartment in *Susan Lenox* add up to more than elements of design. The differences in the way they are meant to be perceived by an audience are palpable. Joan Crawford skitters down a curvilinear staircase without a care and the camera does not linger on any one feature of

An interior view of the moderne penthouse in *Susan Lenox*.

the art deco décor, as if it is perfectly natural that this young woman should live in such an environment. In *Susan Lenox* the camera glides through the open doors of a New York penthouse almost tentatively, as an audience member in blue-collar America might, a bit overwhelmed as maids carrying trays of hors d'oeuvres sweep past. In 1931 the dream that the average American might attain this level of prosperity seemed, to many, more hopeless than finding the mythical city of El Dorado itself. And the penthouse in *Susan Lenox*, as Rodney remarks in the film, belongs to a "shady politician." At the end of the film, Rodney tells Susan, "Do you know what would happen if you came with me? You'd have to cook, wash, live in a dump. . . ." But Susan leaves the penthouse behind and goes with him.

The use of the Manhattan penthouse as a movie setting paralleled the construction of a series of New York skyscraper residences in the late 1920s along Central Park West, among them the Century, built by Irwin Chanin in the early 1930s; Emory Roth's San Remo, which opened in 1930; and the Beresford, which began construction in 1929. In early skyscraper construction, the walls of a building supported the structure; the taller

The entrance to the penthouse apartment in *Susan Lenox*. Greta Garbo can be seen in the background, standing at the entrance to the terrace.

the structure, the thicker the walls had to be. A sixteen-story building at the beginning of the twentieth century needed walls six feet thick at the base. This need was eliminated with the invention of steel-frame construction, in which a rigid steel skeleton was able to support a building's weight; the outer walls were merely hung from the frame, almost like draperies. As a result, glass windows could become expansive and even serve as outer walls, offering up helicopter views of the Manhattan skyline. Gibbons and Toluboff make splendid use of this innovation. Curving walls of glass envelop the apartment in *Susan Lenox*, and an expansive series of steps, a hallmark of moderne design, raise and lower the living room into a series of platforms.

Not six months after the release of *Susan Lenox*, in April 1932, MGM released *Grand Hotel*, a motion picture that today is almost more myth than film. It was Irving Thalberg's antidote for a box office that was showing the first signs of the Depression. Although the studio had used most of its lengthy talent roster in vaudeville-style review films during the very early talkie period, Thalberg, in a feat of showmanship considered remarkable for its time, decided to produce a dramatic film featuring the first all-star company: Greta Garbo, John Barrymore, Joan Crawford, Wallace Beery, Lionel Barrymore, Lewis Stone, and Jean Hersholt were cast in author Vicki Baum's tale of life inside the corridors of Berlin's luxurious Grand Hotel.

In a spate of books that examined the studio system in the 1980s, *Grand Hotel* was still regarded as the ultimate expression of early MGM house style: "Perhaps the consummate expression of the MGM style during Thalberg's regime," wrote Thomas Schatz in his book *The Genius of the System*. Most of that style can be directly attributed to Cedric Gibbons, who took the film on as his own personal project. The main set, which consisted of the lobby and corridors of the hotel, is not only a sterling example of the moderne style, but it becomes another character in the narrative.

Tension is high when the film opens. Expert, accelerating cross-cutting reveals select members of the cast in individual phone booths located in the hotel lobby. Hersholt, playing

The entrance to MGM's *Grand Hotel* set. The spherical motif of the lobby begins with the revolving door and the circular light fixtures above it. Within, the round reception desk and the curving black-and-white tiles that encircle it suggest almost constant movement. As Lewis Stone observes, "People coming . . . going."

the hotel porter Senf, awaits the birth of his child and phones the hospital in exasperation. Next to him, Otto Kringelein (Lionel Barrymore), a long-suffering clerk, talks about coming to Berlin to see a specialist about "that old trouble of mine . . . he says I won't live much longer. I'm staying at the Grand Hotel. It's the most expensive hotel in Berlin. Even our big boss Mr. Preysing stays here. Someday I'm going to tell him exactly what I think of him."

Preysing (Wallace Beery) has his own problems in the next booth. "If the merger does not go through," he tells his father-in-law, "we are in very bad shape, Papa." A few booths away, Suzette (Rafaela Ottiano), Grusinskaya's (Greta Garbo) maid, is in a lather over her employer: "Madam will not dance today. She did not sleep all night. There is something preying on her mind." Next to her, Baron Von Gaigern (John Barrymore) is plotting a heist.

The editing of this sequence builds to a crackling crescendo until we see Louis Stone, as the mysterious Dr. Otternschlag, sitting in the lobby, rather bored: "Grand Hotel," he sighs. "People coming . . . going . . . nothing ever happens." And then the camera cuts to an establishing shot of guests milling about the hotel entrance that is quickly followed

An interior view of the lobby.

This view of the hotel lobby reveals the grillwork motif that is picked up from the revolving door in the entrance.

by an overhead shot revealing a number of floors rising in a spiral above a circular lobby. The reception desk is also spherical, surrounded by alternating black and white tiles that create a curvilinear checkerboard of pathways. The set will become a metaphor within the narrative, with characters passing each other in the hotel lobby continuously yet never quite connecting. "On *Grand Hotel*," Gibbons told *Film Pictorial* in 1933, "[Director] Edmund Goulding thought we should have a carpet on the floor of the hotel; I thought a check floor spiraling in a circular pattern would be more effective and in keeping with the picture—and as a matter of fact he agreed with me after a while, and was nice enough to mention how right I was when we saw the finished picture."

A corridor in the hotel, where Flaemmchen (Joan Crawford) meets the Baron (John Barrymore), features the moderne décor scheme begun in the lobby.

When Gibbons first met Vicki Baum, she implored him, "For pity's sake, don't make the sets modern." But Gibbons had other ideas. "[Baum] had a specific Berlin Grand Hotel in mind, the kind that a vast number of people have visited themselves. I felt, however, that the old marble and red-plush idea lacked the glamour the story demanded. People want to see the type of hotel they hope to visit, like Kringelein himself, so we compromised a bit, avoiding extreme modernity but glorifying the démodé old hotel a bit for American consumption."

"*Grand Hotel* is no mere setting for the action of a story," Gibbons continued. "Here the sets take the place of an actor—become one of the central figures in a great story. The

Grand Hotel is bigger than all the people that come and go within its walls. We therefore went about designing the sets with the view of bringing the background forward on the same plane as the players. The set is a distinct character. The human characters are important, but in this story the hotel itself is even more so."

Gibbons was also inspired in another way. The only time that audience members forget that they are indeed inside the Grand Hotel is when the camera leads them inside a guest room. In each suite, the characters become paramount and the set recedes, becoming mere background. Garbo's suite is shrouded with heavy, dark curtains, and, while it is possible to pick out a chair here and a lamp there in the other rooms, they are often left

In a direct contrast with the public rooms of the hotel, the guest rooms are not in any way distinctive. This was deliberate, as Gibbons felt the interiors should not offer a distraction from the actors.

as dark as possible, with the surroundings often out of focus. There is no incandescent lighting in these scenes. The focus, instead, is on the characters, and each scene within these guest rooms is composed primarily of close-ups and medium shots with key lights accentuating each actor. These sets stand in sharp contrast to the lobby, corridors, bar, and dining rooms, where every detail is emphasized.

The circular lobby was designed for a twofold reason. The oval reception desk, placed in the center of the lobby, is equidistant from every part of the entrance and can be seen instantly from all directions. The camera, usually limited to 180 degrees of movement, acquires a complete 360-degree scan when placed on the desk. An additional advantage of the circular form is that it also permitted the camera to turn from one group of people to another and keep all of them in sharp focus. Nothing escapes it. It spots a character when he or she enters the revolving doors (another round form) and follows the character to the elevator landing. As Donald Albrecht has noted, the circular motif "acts as a pivot for the curving shots that follow the movement of the film's characters, who travel across the black-and-white floor like pawns in a chess game." The revolving door is styled in steel and glass and decorated with horizontal bands, a singular feature of moderne, which is picked up and curved on the interior walls of the lobby.

The fate that has befallen each of the characters as each one exits the lobby for the last time is indicative of the film's middlebrow uplift. Preysing has killed the Baron, and he exits in handcuffs. Grusinskaya, unaware of her lover the Baron's death, leaves the hotel facing an uncertain future. Kringelein, however, who once worked as an assistant book-keeper for Preysing, exits in triumph, sauntering across the checkerboard floor in top hat and morning coat with Flaemmchen (Joan Crawford), the stenographer who worked for Preysing, as they head for Paris.

Prior to the release of *Grand Hotel*, in February 1932, Gibbons expounded on his ideas regarding the set as character with an article he wrote for *American Cinematographer* magazine, and it revealed his sensitivity and astute understanding of what worked in a film,

> The greatest discretion must be observed by both art director and cinematographer in determining whether any given set can be treated as an actor or a background. The dramatic and psychological requirements of story, characterizations, and scene must all be carefully appraised before the decision is made.
>
> The choice of camera angles is another factor which must be considered in this connection. Certain directors—rightly or wrongly—have a penchant for shooting their long shots through parts of the set, as through a frame. At times, this can prove highly effective, but as a rule it is otherwise, for it is both bad art and bad dramatics. In the first place, it is usually painfully obvious. After all, the camera represents (or should) the eye of the audience, and when we look at a thing, we concentrate our attention on the thing itself, not on such objects as may lie between it and our eyes. If we are in a large room, and our friend approaches, we see him—not the chairs, pillars, or potted palms between us. This same natural habit should guide us in photographing such scenes for a motion picture. Using a part of the set, or deliberate "masking pieces" to frame a long shot may make an individually attractive scene, but it also detracts from the dramatic value of the scene and slows the tempo of the sequence. The only exception, of course, is in instances where it is deliberately intended to call attention to the set—where the set itself is an actor. But even here, this habit of framing action with part of the set must be approached with restraint, for if too frequently repeated, it becomes ineffective and monotonous. Frequently at some point in the story it may serve a legitimate dramatic purpose, but if too many of the receding long shots are treated in the same way, for no dramatic reason, but merely to be arty, the really important shot is emasculated.

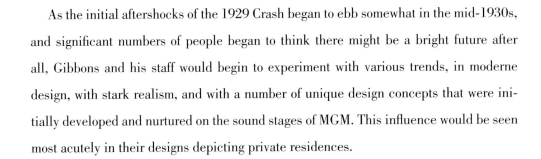

As the initial aftershocks of the 1929 Crash began to ebb somewhat in the mid-1930s, and significant numbers of people began to think there might be a bright future after all, Gibbons and his staff would begin to experiment with various trends, in moderne design, with stark realism, and with a number of unique design concepts that were initially developed and nurtured on the sound stages of MGM. This influence would be seen most acutely in their designs depicting private residences.

CHAPTER SIX

EVERY STAGE A HOME

I N 1933 CEDRIC GIBBONS GAVE HIS MOST FAR-reaching—and certainly one of his longest—interviews, to Mayme Ober Peak of the *Ladies' Home Journal*. Whether intentionally planned by MGM marketing and publicity or not, the discussion would instigate the approach the studio would take when publicizing one aspect of the work its art department would accomplish throughout the next decade. It was a methodology that had been perfected by most of the major Hollywood studios some years previously, when they began to promote costume designers such as Gilbert Adrian at MGM, Travis Banton at Paramount, and Orry-Kelly at Warner Brothers, turning them into American couturiers who could initiate fashion trends. In his *Journal* interview, Gibbons made use of this fashion precedent. "When a woman selects her clothes, she chooses those in which she looks well," he said. "Why not feel the same way about the rooms she lives in?"

Gibbons went on to imply that you didn't need Donald Deskey or Jean-Michel Frank for inspiration if you had the Metro-Goldwyn-Mayer art department:

> A home has much the same decorating problems as a motion picture set. It should be primarily a background for the action that takes place in it and the personalities who live in it. Sets are designed and decorated by experts. Under my supervision is a large staff of architects, designers, and decorators. We have a department where furniture is made and upholstered, drapes made, rugs woven, and pictures framed. We have also a property department, with buyers for it scattered all over the world.
>
> Each picture averages forty sets. Metro-Goldwyn-Mayer studio alone makes fifty-two pictures a year. Unless they are period pictures, which have to be authentic, new ideas are introduced continually.

A major impetus behind this new publicity push was the direct result of two sets Gibbons and his associates designed in 1933 for the films *When Ladies Meet* and *Should Ladies Behave*. Based on a play by Rachel Crothers, *When Ladies Meet* starred Ann Harding, Myrna Loy, Robert Montgomery, and Alice Brady. Loy plays a novelist, Mary Howard, who is working on a book about a love triangle and is not-so-secretly attracted to her married publisher (Frank Morgan). During a weekend getaway at the country house of Mary's friend Bridget Drake (Alice Brady), Mary's ardent suitor, Jimmie (Robert Montgomery), introduces Mary to the publisher's wife, Clare (Ann Harding), without revealing her identity. If the house does not take on the attributes of an actual character in the narrative, like the imposing interiors of the Grand Hotel in Berlin, it is certainly flattered and fawned over by the cast. It was one of the first examples, on-screen or otherwise, of a barn conversion. "Wasn't Walter clever, joining the house onto the barn like that?" Bridget asks Mary soon after she arrives. "Those two rooms," she adds, pointing upward, "used to be used for the hay." Mary can only sigh: "It's so heavenly." Clare is also captivated when she arrives:

The trunk of an actual sycamore tree formed part of the terrace garden of the country house in *When Ladies Meet,* but the branches and leaves were artificial.

Clare: "Oh, this is so lovely."

Bridget: "Yes, it's very sweet, isn't it? Walter made it over from an old barn. Have you ever struggled with an old place, Mrs. Clare?"

Clare: "No, I never have, but I always thought I'd love to."

Clare is then given the "grand tour," which allows the audience an opportunity to see the set in its entirety, and not long after the film's release in the summer of 1933 the mailroom at MGM was flooded with letters from housewives, their husbands, and even architects, all clamoring for blueprints of the set that they could copy. Suddenly, a movie setting was as popular as an Adrian fashion trend. An automobile manufacturer in Detroit

An interior view of the country house in *When Ladies Meet*.

built a replica of the house, as did a businessman in Argentina. Several years later, Gibbons recalled, "It achieved an all-time high for mass interest. It chanced to touch a popular vein and thousands of inquiries came pouring in from people who had never thought of interior design except as something peculiar to Park Avenue alone."

The country house set covered an entire sound stage at MGM and included a large living room, dining room, bathroom, and several bedrooms, all surrounded by a spacious garden. The barn influence was carefully retained with low-beamed ceilings and boarded walls that were painted white as a background for a red, white, and blue color scheme reflected in the draperies and upholstery. Edwin B. Willis, now in charge of set decoration at the studio, found brass and copper lighting fixtures that harmonized with the utensils and fireplace equipment of the Early American period. For all its authenticity, however, it was still a film set. The trunk of an actual sycamore tree formed part of the terrace garden, but the branches and leaves were artificial. Real tile was used for paving the court, but the grass "growing" in its joints was excelsior turf. A "wild wall" made up a section of the living room, constructed so it was easily removable. This allowed the camera to shoot through and around the space. Opposite sides of the room were often not parallel, to afford a wider scope for the camera lens, although the lack of parallelism was not noticeable on the screen. Ceiling molding and millwork, in order to register on camera, was very pronounced.

The sudden return to an idealized and romantic past in 1933 was an abrupt departure from the streamlined moderne sets that Gibbons had been refining and experimenting with in the early years of the 1930s. Still, it clearly resonated with a moviegoing public that may have felt some reassurance in a resurrection of early "Americana" amid the whirlwind of political and economic turmoil that had followed the 1929 Crash. And Gibbons followed his barn conversion set with another, similar set six months later for the film *Should Ladies Behave* with Alice Brady again, this time married to Lionel Barrymore. As in *When Ladies Meet*, the set was not a vital presence in that it neither specifically influenced, inspired, nor shaped the narrative. Brady and Barrymore play an unhappy couple whose daughter becomes infatuated with an older man. Their daughter doesn't realize that her aunt is the man's lover, and everything comes to a head one weekend at the couple's country retreat.

To visualize this retreat, Gibbons entrusted associate art directors Fredric Hope and Harry McAfee with the design and construction of a country estate created in the French provincial style. With a vast lawn of real grass studded with growing trees, plots of live

Above: The French provincial country home created for *Should Ladies Behave.* Note the fleur-de-lis stenciled onto the fireplace mantel.

Right: A long view of Lionel Barrymore's and Alice Brady's country house.

In contrast to the garden created for *When Ladies Meet,* the yard designed for *Should Ladies Behave* featured a lawn of real grass along with growing trees and plots of live flowers.

flowers, and a tennis court, Hollywood, according to an MGM press release for the film, "comes a long stride nearer its apparent destiny of leading the world styles in settings as it now does in fashions."

"Most of the furniture," said Frederic Hope, "is genuine French antique, imported and reupholstered in gay, modern patterns. The copper apron was wrought by a French craftsman here in the studio, as were all of the copper fireplace fittings." The design of the house was more or less authentic, inspired by an old French farmhouse Hope had once visited and studied. "Against a foundation and basic design of pure provincial influence," he said, "we have simply modernized this home, made it cheerful and livable."

By the mid-1930s, Gibbons had begun to champion an offshoot of streamlined moderne that MGM publicity initially labeled "austere elegance," and it made one of its first appearances in the romantic melodrama *Chained*, with Clark Gable and Joan Crawford, in 1934. "Witness the entrance of a fresh note in interior decorations!" proclaimed a feature story that was syndicated to newspapers across the country. The style combined lavishness with severe simplicity. In the New York penthouse that tycoon Richard Field (Otto Kruger) called home, plain whites and cream tones predominated, and the rooms

Even offices received the "austere elegance" treatment in *Chained,* as seen here in Richard Fields's (Otto Kruger) inner sanctum.

were divested of furniture except for a few select pieces. "The new sets," decreed the article, "are expected to attract as much attention as a startling Adrian-designed gown."

New Yorker film critic Pauline Kael once referred to Joan Crawford's mid-1930s vehicles at MGM as "tinseled toys." In hindsight, films such as *Chained*, *Forsaking All Others*, *No More Ladies*, and *I Live My Life*, released during a two-year period between 1934 and 1935, do seem to exist for no other reason than to promote trends in interior design and endorse Crawford as a fashion arbiter. Part of the promotional push for *No More Ladies* suggests as much. Theater owners were provided with ten photos depicting "ultra-smartness, refinement, and dignity—worthy of window display in the highest type of furniture, department or interior decorating store. The furnishings are up to the minute. They're actual production sets designed by Cedric Gibbons for *No More Ladies*— sumptuous scenes for the charm and loveliness of Joan Crawford. Some store could use them for preparation of an illustrated booklet on 'How to Have a Smart House.'" And the feature stories supplied to newspapers across the country took the "austere elegance" of *Chained* one step further:

> Strange as it may seem, the "artistic monstrosities" of yesteryear have marched down from the attic and spare room to set off the fuse to the year's latest styles in interior decorations.
>
> On the Hollywood and New York decorating fronts these styles are called "Neo-Grec," but don't let a word throw you. "New Greek," literally translated, means the old horsehair sofa magically transformed into a thing of modern beauty.
>
> And this automatically puts every owner of furniture from grandma's day in possession of the latest in interior decorations. Hollywood is giving the vogue its greatest impetus in Metro-Goldwyn-Mayer's *No More Ladies*. For this picture Cedric Gibbons, sensing the pulse of the times, bought carloads of family antiques, replaced red plush with creamy satin, gouged out the Victorian gingerbread, slapped on

Interior fluted columns as a decorative device was an important feature of the Neo-Greek style, as seen here in *Forsaking All Others*.

a highly colored paint job—and in all probability will make decorating history.

The new thought in interior decorating, first introduced in a previous Crawford picture, *Forsaking All Others*, caught on at once. Householders with attics full of Victorian, Empire, Napoleonic and Classic furniture followed suit. Fading wallpaper was torn off somber walls and replaced with several coats of white, cream, or yellow paint. Wood trimmings were supplanted by strips of modern metal glass. Dingy rugs were ripped up and fine old floors waxed to a high polish. And "neo-Greek" was born.

Joan Crawford's Neo-Greek country house in *No More Ladies.*

As described in *The Oxford Dictionary of Architecture*, the "Neo" or "New Greek" style combined elements of Greco-Roman classicism with Egyptian revival and Adam style into a "richly eclectic polychrome mélange." The "Adam Style" was named after three Scottish brothers who lived during the eighteenth century and were the first to advocate a cohesive style for architecture and interiors. When awarded a commission, the walls, ceiling, fireplaces, furniture, fixtures, fittings, and carpets were all designed by the Adam Brothers as a single integrated whole. As a set designer, it was a process and philosophy Gibbons could easily embrace.

"New Greek" or "Neo-Classic" as Gibbons now defined it—modern treatment of classic design—reached an apotheosis at MGM in the sets for *Wife vs. Secretary*, in 1935. The plot is summed up in the film's title. The wife (Myrna Loy) of a publishing executive (Clark

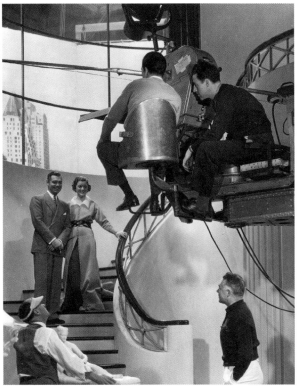

Van and Linda Stanhope (Clark Gable and Myrna Loy) descend the staircase in their Neo-Greek Manhattan penthouse under the watchful eye of director Clarence Brown, in *Wife vs. Secretary*.

Gable) wrongly suspects that her husband is having an affair with his young, attractive secretary (Jean Harlow). The film was touted as being "high voltage" and "ultramodern" in the trailer released to theaters, and Gibbons, working with William Horning and Edwin Willis, designed a duplex Manhattan penthouse for Gable and Loy that lived up to all the publicity.

The apartment represented a month's work in actual construction. The keynote was the sweeping, circular staircase that spilled into the entrance hall, a classical touch set off by a shiny moderne metal rail. Flanking either side of the first few steps were two figures, a crouching ancient Greek maiden and a tall, almost life-size statue of modern design, the complementary symbols of the design concept. A console near the entrance to the breakfast nook held Grecian candlesticks that Gibbons had purchased on a trip to Vienna.

The color scheme in the drawing room was black, brown, and beige. The floor was jet black with a bold white border, and tall windows—always a hallmark of streamlined moderne—lined the length of the room, overlooking a terrace and, ostensibly, Central Park. The Venetian dining room set was all white, and the table was modernized with a mirrored cover.

Above: The entrance to the living room in the penthouse.

Left: The upstairs hallway in the Manhattan penthouse continues the Neo-Greek decorative scheme.

Gibbons's penchant for clean, white surfaces and uncluttered designs with moderne accents is shown here in an ice skating rink created for *Wife vs. Secretary*.

By 1939 and into the early 1940s, Gibbons and his staff would wed early American "traditional" taste with a New Greek point of view in films such as *The Women* and *Susan and God*. Based on the 1936 play by Clare Boothe Luce, *The Women*, released by MGM in 1939, follows the machinations of several Park Avenue society women, chief among them Mary Haines (Norma Shearer), the contented wife of Stephen Haines and mother of Little Mary (Virginia Weidler). Mary is unaware that her husband has been drawn into an affair with a department store salesgirl, Crystal Allen (Joan Crawford), but several women in Mary's social circle make sure she finds out, escalating entanglements in the plot to its ultimate confrontation and denouement.

In contrast to Gable and Loy's penthouse, the secretary in the title, Helen "Whitey" Wilson (Jean Harlow), lives with her parents in a traditional middle-class setting. James Stewart, seated at Harlow's left, plays her boyfriend, Dave.

Audiences first meet Mary Haines at her house in the country, gamboling with her daughter and pets, the veritable picture of domestic serenity. "In designing the sets for *The Women*," said Edwin Willis, "Cedric Gibbons and his staff felt that the home of the heroine, Mary Haines, had to express good taste. She liked nice things, old furniture, fine architecture, as well as the more conservative but still luxuriously modern. Mr. Gibbons and his staff designed the country house under the theory that the couple found an old

CUKOR
PROD. 1091
SET NO.
06
HAINES
LOWER
FLOOR
SC. 22

Above: The wide plank floors used in the country house of Mary Haines (Norma Shearer) in *The Women* is reminiscent of the flooring used in *When Ladies Meet* and *Should Ladies Behave*. Neo-Greek columns can be seen in the entry way, and the Harlequin portrait gives the room a "personal touch."

Right: The living area in the country house from *The Women*.

house dating back as far as 1650. It is one of those places which intelligent remodeling does wonders with, and the heroine wisely restored the fine old features to their original beauty."

In this instance, Gibbons, Willis, and unit art director Wade B. Rubottom went beyond the parameters of the screenplay and executed what amounted to a psychological sketch of an upper-middle-class housewife and mother, rationalizing her design decisions and expounding on the reasons behind them. Willis continued:

> The handsome mantles [sic] were inspired by those described by Nathaniel Hawthorne in *The House of the Seven Gables*. The painting of the little boy Harlequin after the manner of Picasso is the type of thing the heroine might have seen in a gallery and liked. Far from being incongruous, it gives the room just the right personal touch and avoids a general effect that might seem too consciously "decorated" otherwise.
>
> The architecture in the dining room is obviously earlier and was once the great kitchen of the house. This is typical of many old Connecticut houses, when rooms and interior trim were added over a span of several hundred years. The beams and the knee-brace brackets suggest old ship cabin construction.
>
> The decorations were a delight to do. The walls of cream white were an excellent foil for the rich wood tones of the fine old American colonial pieces which our heroine collected, such as the handsome Duncan Phyfe tables, the tilt-top table with the wooden gallery, the primitive Windsor chair, and the unusually fine pedestal table of the Federal period which we used.
>
> The kitchen is about the way our heroine might have found it, with the same crude brick fireplace, oven, and warming ledges. It is now modernized with a sparkling white stove, refrigerator, and the best plumbing. Some of the old utensils still serve the family in our picture. We see the copper pots, old milk jugs, china jars for spices, the brown-glaze bean pots, and other old pottery pieces."

Once shopgirl Crystal Allen (Joan Crawford) steals Mary's husband, Stephen Haines, she remodels the bathroom to suit her own taste. Mary's daughter sums up the décor when she tells her stepmother, "I think this bathroom is perfectly ridiculous!"

For Gibbons, Rubottom, and Willis, the goal in designing this set was to reinforce how hard Mary Haines had worked to create a pleasant, stable, livable environment for her husband and daughter. In contrast, her rival, shopgirl Crystal Allen, lives at the "Hotel Viceroy." The hotel is never seen on screen, but the location alone immediately adds to the image of a transient, unstable character.

The following year, in George Cukor's *Susan and God*, the film version of Rachel Crothers's play, the ultramodern adaptation of the Colonial home was shown to its best advantage. Designed by Gibbons and unit art director Randall Duell, two woods were used in the original finish for the floor and furniture—pine and maple. The furniture, created in the MGM work-rooms, was sealed with a clear lacquer and then sanded and given a coat of yellow wax. The result was a glowing patina the color of strained honey. Various surfaces were then slightly mutilated—scarred by hand—to simulate the wear of over 150 years. The bright red and white chintz patterns on the sofas were inspired by early Colonial designs. The dining room table was a type found in the dining quarters of early American clipper ships; the leaves are supported by a form of butterfly bracket so they fold down when not in use. As MGM publicity noted, it is a good note for the housewife of today to remember, especially if she lives in a boxlike apartment where every speck of space is at a premium.

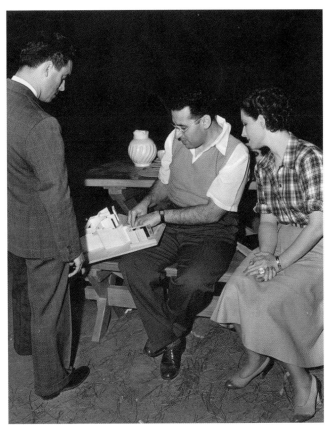

Although many accounts of Gibbons's career maintain that his word was law at MGM, in actuality directors had a good deal of input regarding the sets for their films. Here George Cukor makes an adjustment to a set model for *The Women* as Norma Shearer looks on.

The desire to make "decorating history," however, did not preclude the creation of interior sets that reflected and supported both the characters and narrative of a film. One of the best examples is David O. Selznick's production of *Dinner at Eight* in 1933. Director George Cukor requested the services of New York interior decorator Hobe Erwin, who would work alongside MGM designer Fredric Hope. While all the action in *Grand Hotel* took place in its suites, public rooms, and lobby, *Dinner at Eight* scrutinizes the

Kitty Packard's (Jean Harlow) dressing table in *Dinner at Eight*. According to interior decorator Hobe Erwin, it indicated "to what extent wealth may be combined with bad taste."

A close-up view of Kitty Packard's dressing table reveals the pains set decorators such as Edwin Willis took to create a realistic setting that also reflected the personality of the character in the film.

lives of five main characters and moves from one location to another, among them Lionel Barrymore and Billie Burke's Park Avenue apartment, Jean Harlow's pseudomodernistic boudoir, John Barrymore's hotel suite, and the executive offices of Lionel Barrymore's shipbuilding firm. Of the lot, Erwin considered Harlow's boudoir to be the most interesting, as it indicated "to what extent wealth may be combined with bad taste." Ten different shades of white were used for this room, fresh-white chiffon for glass curtains, oyster-white satin for drapes, lacquer-white for a wardrobe with ornamentation of dead chalk-white, cream-white for the velvet walls, milk-white for the chenille rug, and an ivory taffeta for the bedspread. Another highlight of the room was a chaise lounge in squares of a warmer white.

"It sounds like a ghastly combination," said Erwin, "but there are many different tones of white, and properly mixed they can give you an illusion of not one color but many colors. In this instance, however, the idea was to present a setting which would give the observer an insight into its occupant, namely the pretty but common Kitty Packard [played by Jean Harlow], wife of a nouveau riche millionaire. . . . The audience will take one look at this room and then will have little difficulty in recognizing the character of the person who would live in it." The many white fleur-de-lis that adorned Harlow's bed and dressing table, a symbol of the Bourbon monarchy in France and here rendered in feathers, certainly underscored the point.

An interior setting could "act" in other ways, too, and one of the best examples can be found in Gibbons's designs for *Another Thin Man*, the third sequel to the long-running series of films that began with *The Thin Man*, starring William Powell and Myrna Loy, in 1934. This film begins when an elderly New York financier is murdered on his Long Island estate. The financier's home might have been anything from modern to prim colonial, but after studying the script, Gibbons decided to make the surroundings conform to the grim nature of the crime itself. He was inspired to furnish the home with fixtures and furniture from one of the most somber periods in the history of American design—what

Gibbons referred to as the "General Grant period," an American interpretation of Victorian interiors.

"It was a period when dark woods were used almost exclusively for furniture," said Gibbons, "and the heavier and more forbidding the furniture the more highly it was prized. House interiors were gloomy because windows were small and, anyway, the curtains were always drawn because sunlight faded the rugs."

To accentuate the gloominess, Gibbons designed the walls of the home with "funereal bands," black moldings at top and bottom, and held the wall colors to dreary grays and monochromatic tans. Obtaining enough furniture from this period to furnish the ten rooms required by the screenplay was a difficult task, as very little of it had survived once the vogue had passed. Gibbons was able to collect only a dozen chairs, a couple of tables, and a mantelpiece. Furniture from most other periods of design was easily duplicated in the studio workshops. This period furniture from the 1870s was so elaborately carved, however, that few cabinetmakers were familiar enough with the style. But the motto of the MGM art department was, "It can't be done, but here it is," and lathes and jigsaws went to work, using the genuine antiques as models. Nearly fifty pieces were completed before the start of filming, and while the set was not for a psychological thriller along the lines of *The Spiral Staircase* or *Night Must Fall*, this set for *Another Thin Man* achieved its purpose: placing Nick and Nora Charles in a forbidding atmosphere, where a heavy curtain or a hallway clogged with heavy furniture and dark shadows might anticipate any number of threats.

Some of this furniture was reused to create a similar effect for the interior of No. 9 Thornton Square in London for George Cukor's *Gaslight*, with Ingrid Bergman and Charles Boyer. "Those sets are an example of the resources of a big studio," Cukor remarked many years later. "I don't think we had to go out and get any of the pieces of the period; they were all there." The exterior streets representing Thornton Square had been built on the backlot ten years previously for *The Barretts of Wimpole Street* and consisted of two

What Gibbons referred to as the "General Grant" period of interior design was used for the Long Island mansion of a financier in *Another Thin Man*.

A suitably ominous atmosphere created for an upstairs hallway in the mansion from *Another Thin Man*.

The interior of the townhouse where Gregory and Paula (Charles Boyer and Ingrid Bergman) return to live twenty years after the murder of Paula's aunt on the premises.

sides of a nineteenth-century British square, gaslit with four-story garret-topped buildings fronting on a park enclosed by a high, wrought-iron fence.

"The film's sets were exceptionally beautiful," remembered Cukor, "and a lot of the decoration—for which we had the advice of Paul Huldschinsky, a refugee who had been very rich in Germany and who had enormous taste—was modeled on Punch and

Du Maurier drawings of the period. They gave us a great deal of the proper late-Victorian atmosphere, as well as an interesting visual quality." And also, at the beginning, an evocative sense of dread. When Paula (Ingrid Bergman) and Gregory (Charles Boyer) return to live at No. 9, twenty years after the murder of Paula's aunt on the premises, they find an interior stuffed with furniture shrouded in dustcloths and chandeliers encircled in netting. Countless curios and souvenirs are crammed into ancient bureaus, and dozens of framed paintings, drawings, and mementoes are affixed to fading wallpaper. "It's all dead in here," Paula tells her husband when they arrive. "The whole place seems to smell of death." After the couple renovate, the set for the crowded London drawing room where much of the film takes place included a pair of Cornucopia sofas, in tufted satin and

The townhouse restored, with the two Cornucopia sofas in the foreground.

The attic set in *Gaslight* where Paula finally confronts Gregory.

the only ones of their kind in the United States at that time, as well as a piano on which Charles Boyer accompanies Bergman. It was discovered at auction at an English country estate and was fashioned entirely out of one piece of rosewood. The sets won Academy Awards for Gibbons, unit art director William Ferrari, and for Edwin B. Willis and Paul Huldschinsky for set decoration.

In 1941, eight years after the release of *When Ladies Meet*, MGM cast Joan Crawford, Robert Taylor, and Greer Garson in a remake of the original film. In this version, the country retreat was said to be converted from an old mill and is introduced to viewers with a slow-moving panoramic traveling shot. A huge waterwheel was employed to fill up the swimming pool, which looks like a natural pond. The interior, however, is a replication of the original set. Actually, it may very well be the original. When Fredric Hope was escorting visiting architect Elmer Gray around MGM in 1933, Gray inquired as to the necessity of the gutters and downspouts on the set. He was told that the studio might someday wish to move the set outdoors to use again, in which case moderate precautions against rain would be desirable.

Gibbons found that the set still resonated with audiences, for it surpassed the previous fan mail record set by the first film in 1933. People wrote in from all over the country requesting either blueprints or information as to where they could buy a specific lamp seen in the den or a rug on the floor of the living room. A 1942 article in *House Beautiful* noted, "Cedric Gibbons and Ed Willis, the men who designed these sets, say the rooms were popular because most people want the clean-cut simplicity and usableness [*sic*] of modern design, bright color, and bold patterns, yet still love the familiar warmth and romanticism of the past. These rooms crystallize these mixed desires so subtly that in one over-all atmosphere you feel Early American has lost its inconvenience for modern comfort, while modern has been stripped of its starkness, given heart and traditional charm."

Elizabeth Gordon, publisher of *House Beautiful*, sent a preliminary mock-up of this article to Gibbons, accompanied by her own example of "fan mail." In a letter dated May 27, 1942, Gordon wrote:

> I am enclosing a paste-up of an article which will appear in the summer issue of *House Beautiful*.
>
> I wonder if you can tell me where you obtained the rug on the floor of the living room. We are fascinated by it and would like to know if it is available to us as a prop on some of our decorating jobs. Is it the property of Metro-Goldwyn-Mayer, or is it something you borrowed as a prop from some Los Angeles resource?
>
> I am expecting to be in Los Angeles for 10 days or 2 weeks beginning around June 11 or 12, and I should like very much to meet you and to find out what future plans you have for building sets as lovely

as this one for *When Ladies Meet*. I should like to run more material of yours of this sort and should like to know your plans enough in advance so that we can schedule the photographs at the time the movie breaks.

The rug, as it turned out, was handmade and purchased on special order from a Mrs. T. H. Thurlow who lived not far from Gibbons in Santa Monica. Although he was happy to escort Elizabeth Gordon around the MGM art department and backlot when she visited the studio, nothing would come of her offer. MGM had its own outlets for publicizing the fashions and settings used in its films.

Sixty-two years later, in November 2004, the editors at *House Beautiful* interviewed noted New York interior designer Susan Zises Green as part of its annual feature on the nation's top 125 decorators. When asked about some of the influences on her design philosophy, she replied, "I love *The Women* with Norma Shearer, Joan Crawford, Rosalind Russell, Joan Fontaine, and Paulette Goddard. The sophistication, elegance, and perfection of style in the pre- and post-war era inspire me tremendously. The sets and costumes are sumptuous, elegant, and full of Old Guard chic." The interior designs conceived in the art department at Metro-Goldwyn-Mayer continue to galvanize designers into the twenty-first century.

CHAPTER SEVEN

RE-CREATING THE WORLD FOR MGM

I N HIS BOOK *MAYER AND THALBERG*, MGM STORY editor Samuel Marx related an incident that occurred between Cedric Gibbons and Irving Thalberg in 1926. Gibbons had objected to the final script of a film titled *Paris*. It was set, as the title suggested, in the French capital. The script called for a love scene to be enacted against the background of an ocean flooded with moonlight. Gibbons visited Thalberg's office and confronted him with a sheaf of photographs that demonstrated the city of Paris was not located anywhere near a large body of water. "We can't cater to a handful of people who know Paris," was Thalberg's response. "Audiences only see about ten per cent of what's on the screen anyway, and if they are watching your backgrounds instead of my actors the scene will be useless. Whatever you put there, they'll believe that's how it is." When the picture was released, Thalberg asked Gibbons if he had received any letters pointing out the discrepancy. He had to admit that he had not. "That proves I'm right," said Thalberg, "but it doesn't prove you're wrong." He urged Gibbons to continue to disagree with him. "The last thing I need is flattery!"

But with the advent of "talkies" in a few short years and the addition of dialogue, an element that bestowed a jolt of naturalism into narrative films, Gibbons began to develop a mania for realism, particularly in films that took place in specific historical time periods. He started to persuade Thalberg to organize a research department on the lot that would delve into and collect information regarding the accuracy of both settings and costumes in MGM productions. Gibbons had a powerful ally in William Randolph Hearst, who in 1922 took the issue of accuracy so seriously that he employed Harold Hendee, described by *Collier's* as "a scholar of some distinction," to see to it that the sets and props of *When Knighthood Was in Flower* and *Janice Meredith* (1924) were faithfully rendered. Hendee later headed up the research department at RKO Studios. Thalberg finally acquiesced. The fact that in the early 1930s he was planning literary adaptations and historical subjects as conceivable screen vehicles for his wife, Norma Shearer, may have influenced his decision. The publication of the Payne Fund Studies in 1934, along with the stringent enforcement of the Hays Code that same year, also led MGM and other Hollywood studios to look increasingly to the classics for screen material.

The person who was chosen to organize and oversee this new department at MGM had begun work there in 1927 as a script reader, and her background could have been the source of a hair-raising adventure film made right on the backlot. Nathalie Bucknall was born into the Russian nobility in 1895; her father, Ivan de Fedenko, was Counsellor of State to Tsar Nicholas II. During the 1917 October Revolution, she found asylum at the British Embassy, later marrying George Bucknall of the Royal Naval Volunteer Reserve. At the end of World War I, Nathalie joined the front lines, defending the Winter Palace against Bolshevik forces. Later she joined an Imperial Red Cross organization where she was influential in setting up hospital facilities for British and White Russian forces operating in the Caucasus. She made her way to England in 1919, where she revealed the whereabouts of classified documents that had belonged to a British officer who was

Nathalie Bucknall (left), head of the MGM research department, shows actress Elizabeth Allen some of the material the department collected for the 1935 production of *David Copperfield*.

murdered at the embassy during the revolution. For this Nathalie was awarded the Order of the British Empire for "special services" to the Crown.

By the time the Bucknalls made their way to Los Angeles in 1926, Nathalie spoke Russian, English, French, and German fluently and had a working knowledge of Swedish, Norwegian, Spanish, and Italian. Blessed with a photographic memory and extensive knowledge of such pertinent topics as architecture, fashion, and world cultures, Nathalie was often referred to at MGM as "the Woman Who Knows All" and still later came to be called "Hollywood's Walking Encyclopedia."

Russian icons, hung correctly according to Nathalie Bucknall's instructions, in Greta Garbo's boudoir from *Anna Karenina*.

Her influence and her importance to any production can be seen in the fact that she was allowed onto any closed set at any hour of the day. This included a bolted Stage 27 in 1935, where director Clarence Brown was filming *Anna Karenina* with the reclusive Greta Garbo on sets that were both blocked and barricaded from the intrusive eyes of onlookers. During one visit, Nathalie remembered, she noted that Russian icons in the film used as set dressing were scattered about the walls like paintings when they should have been placed in a specific corner of the room by themselves. "Otherwise," she laughed, "all would be well until some elderly Russian on Second Avenue in New York writes in his native language to inquire, "Who is that ignorant one in Tolstoy's *Anna Karenina* who hangs icons on the wall as if they were pictures?"

Far more complex, and under Gibbons's direct jurisdiction, was the construction of three railroad stations for the film as they existed in Russia in the late nineteenth century and a full mile of railroad tracks and spurs that had to be built on the backlot. The stations were copied from authentic prints and photographs of the time collected by the research department. In the studio's shops, seven passenger coaches in the characteristic colors of the Russian Empire—red, blue, and orange—were constructed, along with six freight cars. "The classics," Bucknall commented later that year, "have more than tripled the demands on the research department. Each production of a classic has set a new peak in demands for information that frequently necessitates a wide-world search. Before the classics, 300 requests a week was considered a high figure. Now we have more requests than that in a day."

One of the first literary adaptations Thalberg planned for his wife was a film version of *The Barretts of Wimpole Street*, Rudolf Besier's play about the courtship of Elizabeth Barrett and the poet Robert Browning. There were no photos taken during the Barretts' occupancy of No. 50 Wimpole Street in the 1840s, as photography was still in its infancy, but the research department was able to procure floor plan sketches of the house, which in 1934 was in use as a physician's office. Description and detail were supplied by Elizabeth Barrett herself, in letters that had been recently published and were written while she lived at No. 50 as an invalid. In a letter dated May 26, 1843, Barrett wrote to a friend, "No, you would certainly never recognize my prison if you were to see it. The bed, like a sofa and no bed; the large table placed out in the room, towards the wardrobe end of it; the sofa rolled where a sofa should be rolled—opposite the armchair; the doors crowned with a coronal of shelves fashioned to carry my books; the washing table opposite turned into a cabinet with another coronal of shelves; and Chaucer's and Homer's busts on guard over the two departments of English and Greek poetry." From these details, Gibbons was able to build a set for the film that no preview audience could criticize. The box office success of *The Barretts of Wimpole Street* would see an increasing number of literary

Above: The Moscow train station re-created for *Anna Karenina*.

Right: The desk belonging to Anna's son Sergei (Freddie Bartholomew) in *Anna Karenina*. Although almost unnoticeable in the background of the scene in which it appears, the desk features authentic Russian books and toys from the period.

Elizabeth Barrett's bedroom, complete with bust and rolled sofa as described in her letter.

properties and historical subjects go before the cameras at MGM, including *Queen Christina*, *Treasure Island*, *The Gorgeous Hussy*, *A Tale of Two Cities*, *David Copperfield*, *Mutiny on the Bounty*, and in the 1940s, *The Picture of Dorian Gray* and *Pride and Prejudice*.

To build the HMS *Bounty*, Gibbons and unit art directors James Havens and Arnold Gillespie used an exact scale of the original *Bounty* drawings from the British admiralty. In order to accommodate location filming on the Isthmus of Catalina Island, equipment was transported from MGM by the "*Bounty*" itself and two barges towed by tugs. This included two generating plants, two boom trucks, several automobiles, studio lamps, props, a hundred-foot Tahitian war canoe, fifteen outriggers, forty breadfruit trees, eight interior studio sets, and a dozen or more huge baskets of wardrobe, cameras, and electrical equipment. It's no wonder that Thalberg preferred to shoot everything on the backlot whenever possible.

For *Queen Christina* (1933), Greta Garbo's first film under her new contract with MGM, signed in 1932, the star became a virtual adjunct of the research department. On an extended vacation in Sweden, Garbo researched the life of the seventeenth-century Swedish queen she was to portray, visiting the site of Christina's abdication, a castle in Uppsala, as well as various museums and archives. According to MGM head of publicity Howard Strickling, "the sketches she made proved invaluable." And Garbo herself soon realized how invaluable the research department and MGM's legions of craftspeople would be to a film that was a personal project for her. Although her confidant and sometime screenwriter Salka Viertel had urged Garbo to make *Christina* in Europe, Garbo reluctantly declined, writing that "Metro was the best studio and Thalberg the most capable producer to deal with," and explaining further that there were "technical as well as emotional reasons why the film could not be made abroad."

Garbo made numerous sketches of the imposing castle at Uppsala, but Bucknall and her associates discovered that forty years after Christina had abdicated the throne the building was completely destroyed in a fire. A new royal residence was constructed soon afterward, but no paintings or sketches remained of the old castle. Accordingly, the research department found it necessary to access a number of travel diaries from the period for descriptions of the interiors and to follow with fidelity the architectural floor plans found in a volume of royal records. With some imagination added, this information enabled Gibbons and unit art director Alexander Toluboff to reconstruct the façade and walls of the palace as it looked on its steep hill, as well as the throne room, the diet room, Christina's bedroom, and the reception chamber.

Most of the buildings in seventeenth-century Sweden consisted of stone and wood— massive stone walls and huge carved wooden furniture. The exceptional bulk and solidity required made it impossible to use anything from the large prop warehouse maintained by MGM, so an unprecedented amount of skilled manual labor was imperative before the picture could begin. The stone used in construction was "aged" by a special painting

Above: The council room in Christina's palace. Much of the heavy furniture typical of the period was handmade in the MGM workrooms.

Left: A corridor of the palace created for *Queen Christina.*

The special process of "muddying" can be seen in this set from *Queen Christina*. It made the stone walls in the palace appear aged and worn.

process known as "muddying." When applying oils to a surface that is already covered with wet paint, the colors mix and eventually "muddy," creating a softening effect. In addition, all of the outside woodwork used in the film received a coating of bluish tint to impart the feeling of northern chill. Actual timber was used for the logs in the inn and the construction was accurately done with moss and oakum, a preparation of tarred fiber used to seal gaps. It was traditionally used in shipbuilding during this period, for caulking or packing the joints of timbers in wooden vessels.

Closer to home, Gibbons's own acumen proved extremely useful when designing sets for Clarence Brown's production of *The Gorgeous Hussy*, starring Joan Crawford, in 1936. The film was based on the life of Peggy O'Neal (1796–1879), the daughter of William O'Neal, an Irish immigrant and the owner of a boardinghouse and tavern, the Franklin House, on I Street in Washington DC. In 1829 Peggy O'Neal married John Henry Eaton, US secretary of war under President Andrew Jackson. The wives of the other cabinet members refused to accord her social recognition, partly because of her humble birth.

"Historic, architectural gems that dot the South and are in a state of perfect preservation proved the inspiration for the many authentic sets we created for *The Gorgeous Hussy*," said Gibbons upon completion of the film. "The finest brick architecture in the world, typically American, was developed in the South and Washington in the early years of the nineteenth century."

Lionel Barrymore and Joan Crawford as Andrew Jackson and Peggy O'Neal Eaton in *The Gorgeous Hussy*.

Several years prior to taking the film into production, Gibbons had spent time in Washington, Maryland, Virginia, and the Carolinas, making notes and taking photographs of interesting homes and public buildings, adding them to files in the research department in the hope of one day re-creating them for the screen. For six months prior to the beginning of production, the MGM art department collected data for the sets. Gibbons and his associates on the film, William Horning and Edwin Willis, did not attempt to design actual homes but to present a complete picture of the architecture of the time, with its striking dignity and simplicity of line. In one large set, representing an early

The taproom in the Franklin Inn re-created for *The Gorgeous Hussy*.

nineteenth-century street in the nation's capital, buildings inspired by those found in Richmond, Charleston, and Annapolis can be seen.

For the Franklin House, as it is seen in the film, Gibbons and Horning sought inspiration for exteriors in inns found in Richmond and Annapolis, and the taproom in the hostelry was taken from an inn that still existed in Georgetown. The drawing room was adapted from a similar room preserved in the Metropolitan Museum. Two of the bedrooms were inspired by a home in Charleston, which in 1936 had remained untouched for more than a hundred years. In every instance, candlesticks, brass reflectors, brass locks, fixtures, the Franklin stove, and other accessories were duplicated in the MGM shops using the originals as models.

Assigning photographers to make extensive records of architectural styles that had to be duplicated on MGM sound stages became a common practice at the studio by the mid-1930s. For David O. Selznick's productions of *A Tale of Two Cities*, starring Ronald Colman, and *David Copperfield* (both 1935) cameramen were dispatched throughout France and England to find examples of inns and houses of the period that had sustained little to no alteration. Old relics such as doorknobs and samples of old wallpaper were purchased and shipped to the studio to be used or duplicated. Dickens's passion for intimate description was a tremendous assistance to Gibbons and unit art director Fredric Hope. The author often paused in his narratives to delineate a period's style in furnishings, tableware, and clothing. Director George Cukor and Selznick himself undertook their own research trip before taking *David Copperfield* into production, visiting the old Sun Inn in Canterbury, England. It was in this inn, then called the Little Inn, that David and the Micawber family were reunited. Dickens once stayed in this hotel that, as it happens, was completely refurbished in 2006 and still welcomes guests. Based on photographs that Cukor and Selznick took, the inn was reconstructed on the backlot.

Traveling the globe as a research assistant or photographer for MGM, however, might not be the unalloyed delight—or adventure—that a person might think. The following

CUKOR-781
SET No. 8146
INT. OF Suml
Inn Room

CUKOR-781
SET No. 8101

Above: A re-creation of the Little Inn from *David Copperfield.*

Right: This English street on the backlot, with leaded casement windows and timbered roofs, was used in both *A Tale of Two Cities* and *David Copperfield.*

letter was sent by set decorator Hugh Hunt to Gibbons while on a research trip for a film version of Rudyard Kipling's *Kim*, which would ultimately not go before the cameras until 1950:

Letter from Hugh Hunt to Gibbons
Taj Mahal Hotel
Bombay, India
May 23, 1937

I have enclosed invoice on first shipment of goods that will arrive in Los Angeles on July 25, quickest possible time from here. I have tagged pieces I wish quantity made from.

One runs up against many tough problems here, so many in fact to narrate them would take weeks. People only work four or five hours here and have only one speed when going, reverse. Doing the very best I can as you know.

Man is it hot, only 104 here in Bombay, but where I am leaving for tonight, LaHore, it is 128 and no shade, some fun. I hope they keep the starting date off until these things reach the studio. Excuse me while I get another block of ice to sit on.

This "shipment of goods" and many others were housed in a four-story building equipped with a service elevator near the art department. The fourth floor contained period reproductions made in the studio workrooms. Descending the stairs to the second and third floors, one found a second collection of modern and Early American furniture, some genuine pieces and some handsome copies. The first floor contained all manner of bric-a-brac. China occupied aisle after aisle, most of it ordinary, for unless it was high-lighted for a specific reason it rarely garnered attention in a film. Row upon row of lamps, from the sublime to the ridiculous, were open to view. Rugs were piled on shelf following shelf. A truck parked in a corner of the room carried current and past automobile license plates from every state in the union. A jewelry shop was lodged in another corner, and behind the building was a garage with every known type of jalopy, wagon, limousine, and go-cart. All of this property was under the supervision of Edwin Willis.

In the late 1930s Willis himself would be sent on several fact- and artifact-seeking trips, as MGM prepared to mount a number of lavish productions, all of them under the guiding hand of Irving Thalberg. The first of these he referred to as "the fulfillment of a long-cherished dream": a film version of Shakespeare's *Romeo and Juliet*. Louis B. Mayer was initially opposed to the film, stating that "the masses don't understand Shakespeare," but Thalberg appealed to Nicholas Schenck, the president of Loew's Inc. and the man who ultimately controlled the purse strings. He approved a budget of eight hundred

Edwin Willis unpacks a box of imported furniture that will be used in *Marie Antoinette*.

Part of the fourth floor in the MGM property storeroom.

thousand dollars, which eventually ballooned to more than two million dollars. Thalberg saw the film as the apotheosis of Norma Shearer's acting talent and her status as the "First Lady of the Screen," a title MGM publicity had conferred on her in 1934.

To accomplish this, George Cukor was hired to direct, and, as he had done before with *Dinner at Eight*, he championed the hiring of an outside designer, Oliver Messel, to create both the sets and costumes. Messel was one of Britain's foremost film and stage designers and had recently designed the costumes for Alexander Korda's film version of *The Scarlet Pimpernel*, which established Merle Oberon as an international star. As might be expected, Messel's hiring was not greeted with enthusiasm by Gibbons or MGM costume designer Gilbert Adrian, who told Mayer, "Don't think I'm just the MGM workhorse, because I'm not. I'm the MGM designer. If *Romeo and Juliet* is an MGM picture,

I am designing it." This led Shearer to make a judicious decision. She obviously knew that she would be working with Adrian again as long as she remained at MGM, and he had already been designing her costumes for eight years. Messel had only been hired to design this one film. For Shearer, there really was no decision to make. Messel wound up designing half of the women's costumes. Adrian would design the other half, and Norma Shearer's gowns as well.

Thalberg decided that Gibbons and Messel would also divide their tasks when designing the sets. Messel would be billed in the credits as an "artistic consultant," and Gibbons soon dispatched him to Verona and other sites in Italy with two camera crews, where he spent months taking photographs of buildings, plazas, squares, paintings, and frescoes. As planning got underway, the production established a new research record when, in one day, more than three hundred requests were received by Nathalie Bucknall for material on such subjects as bubonic plague, falcons, rapier and dagger fighting, fifteenth-century Italian costumes, Veronese churches, Renaissance furniture, burial ceremonies, and period musical instruments, to name a few. During the process, Bucknall discovered information

Oliver Messel painting a set model for *Romeo and Juliet*.

that surprised even the studio's research head. The bagpipe, always thought of as a Scottish instrument, was played in Verona long before it "skirled" to inspire tartan-clad Caledonians to battle.

When Messel returned from Italy, Gibbons fitted 2,769 scale photographs taken from every conceivable angle into a mosaic to construct a pictorial map of Verona that depicted all of the city's remaining medieval and Renaissance structures. Using this map as a guide, and with assistance from Fredric Hope and Messel, Gibbons built three miniature

After fifty-four models were created of Verona Square in the MGM art department, this was the final result, built on the backlot.

Veronas to scale in three distinct styles—one inch to three feet. One was highly stylized in a sort of abstract mood, one realistically medieval, and another equally realistic but in the early Renaissance period that Messel preferred. There were fifty-four models, and when they were completed, even to the coloring of tile and tiny stained-glass windows, they went to the sketch artists who proceeded to turn out scores of large drawings illustrating possible camera angles.

Gibbons decided to make the exteriors realistic and authentic but inclining toward the medieval. He felt that the interiors depicted, however, should reveal a later period of design, reasoning that a wave of building and remodeling must have swept over Italy during the Renaissance and would have had its effect upon both the Montagues and the

The interior of the Capulets' home, where Gibbons decided to use features of Gothic architecture, such as semicircular arches.

Capulets and the lavish homes in which they lived. According to Gibbons, for this reason the ballroom in the Capulet Palace was probably the one setting in which the greatest license was taken.

> Architects usually date the Renaissance from Brunelleschi and his Dome of the Cathedral in Florence. (1379–1446). Broadly, we may term the Capulet home as Renaissance though the exterior is considerably earlier. Social life during the Renaissance centered around the home rather than the church as it had the preceding period. Therefore, the severe medieval architecture was either demolished or altered to fit the new more material and less spiritual ideas of the social arts which in the Renaissance gave such a tremendous impetus to the admiration and desire for luxury and display.
>
> The design for the setting for the Capulet ballroom permits to the fullest the recreation of the pomp splendor and magnificence of the Renaissance. The setting is two hundred feet long and 60 feet wide. Its lighting is from torches and not from the artificial light which would be necessary in a stage production. While there was no evidence of such a room in Verona nevertheless there is no reason why such a room could not have been built and lived in, or, as our picture requires, danced in.

The ornate, flowered garlands that were hung atop the high arched walls of the ballroom were a characteristic Messel design motif, and this was also reflected in the design for Juliet's bedroom. Some critics felt that Messel's romantic vision of fifteenth-century Italy was in conflict with Gibbons's medieval stylings, creating a disjointed atmosphere. But from a historical point of view, it made perfect sense to appreciate the fact that any urban area would feature an accumulation of architectural styles over time. Although the film seems calcified now, more determined to turn a literary classic into a film classic on its own terms and negating the undercurrent of hot passion underneath, the beauty of many of its sets remains undiminished.

The Capulet ballroom had a Renaissance feel. The flowered garlands atop the high-arched walls were a characteristic Oliver Messel design motif.

Two of the films Thalberg planned in his final years would necessitate numerous trips to France and a buying spree that would remain unsurpassed in the history of the studio. One began with a "succinct little memo" that was sent from Thalberg's office to Nathalie Bucknall early in 1934: "Please prepare some intimate research material on Marie Antoinette." Miss Bucknall called in her staff, telephoned for reserves, and said, "Well, it looks like we're in at the birth of another epic." *Marie Antoinette*, again starring Thalberg's wife, Norma Shearer, would not go into production until a year after the producer's untimely death in 1936. But as Shearer told biographer Gavin Lambert in 1973, "He was dead, but it was still his."

Hunt Stromberg, the unit producer who had been assigned to the film following Thalberg's death, obtained permission from the French government to photograph the Palace

Above: Director George Cukor, seated on a camera dolly, lines up a shot with Norma Shearer on the Capulet ballroom set.

Left: The apothecary shop in *Romeo and Juliet* is a testament to both the research and art departments at Metro-Goldwyn-Mayer.

of Versailles for the first time as a motion picture background. From the hundreds of photographs that were obtained, reproductions were made of the Versailles chapel, grand stairway and hall, the ballroom, the gardens surrounding the Petit Trianon, the royal apartments of Louis XVI and Marie Antoinette, and even the secret stairway where Marie Antoinette met the dashing Count Axel von Fersen.

Taken from construction department requisitions, materials that went into the sets included 80,000 feet of lumber, 25,000 feet of flooring, 90,000 square feet of plaster, 16,000 feet of composition board, 9 tons of structural steel, 400 barrels of paint, 12 gallons of gilt, 120 books of gold leaf, 42 barrels of varnish, and 60 kegs of nails. An acre of real grass was grown on Stage 28 for the gardens that surrounded the Petit Trianon gardens.

Set dressing of the interiors was carried out with equal care. E. B. Willis, head of the property department, purchased seven truckloads of furniture, antiques, and art objects in Paris. In the record shipment were furnishings from the Louis XIV, XV and XVI periods, original Aubusson carpets, Beauvais tapestries, brocades, Sevres and Meissen porcelains, crystal chandeliers, ormolu clocks, an initialed Antoinette chair from the Petit Trianon, and other museum pieces. To this day it retains the record for the largest number of antiques ever received at the port of Los Angeles at one time. And when Willis could find only one left of a certain type of antique from the period and it was not for sale, such as a gilt bronze Louis XV lantern that hung in the entrance hall to the queen's staircase, he had duplicates made from photographs.

W. S. Van Dyke II, the director Mayer assigned to the project, noted that from a marketing standpoint, "the picture would have to be done with an extraordinary degree of authenticity and strict attention to detail for European audiences are very critical." Despite the attention to detail of baroque and rococo design, liberties were taken with history. The grand staircase that appears in the film was actually demolished at Versailles in 1752, eighteen years before Marie arrived at the chateau from Vienna, and the

A façade of Versailles with waiting carriages from *Marie Antoinette*. Many of the carriages were constructed in the studio's workrooms.

A set representing the shop where Louis XVI and Marie Antoinette were discovered and arrested as they attempted to flee France in a carriage.

Above: A re-creation of Louis XV's throne room, where he welcomes the young Marie Antoinette to France. Note the baby spots on each pillar in the foreground. The dustcloths were meant to prevent scuffing between takes.

Right: The prison beneath the Tuileries Palace in Paris where Marie was held prior to her execution. These props were viewed only fleetingly on-screen in a traveling shot.

ballroom never existed at the actual palace. Balls and other fêtes, such as those given to celebrate the marriage of the Dauphin, were almost always held in the Hall of Mirrors.

For his part Gibbons told the *New York Times* that his chief problem was to create a Versailles in which a moving picture could be shot, and in this one instance the research provided inspiration rather than a guidepost to completely authentic replication. "The principal requirements were a ballroom, an entrance hall and a grand staircase—none of which owe anything to the original," he said. He was actually quite unapologetic in his attitude toward the palace—describing it as "a fright," and stating for the record that his sets are better architecturally as well as cinematically than the place they are supposed to represent. He expected to get numerous letters chiding him and Metro for

The ballroom set, which was meant to stand in for the Hall of Mirrors at Versailles.

A cutaway ceiling reveals the klieg lights illuminating the ballroom.

the monumental ignorance of their supposed architectural model displayed in the court sequences, but the exact opposite occurred. The French government presented Gibbons with a special award for his designs. But Gibbons's honesty about the architecture of Versailles has been corroborated by at least one noted source. In her biography of Louis XIV, *The Sun King*, Nancy Mitford wrote, "No doubt Versailles held some special charm for him; the courtiers never could figure out what it was."

◇

For *Camille*, another Thalberg production set in France, many of the properties and much of the furniture used in the settings also came from Europe or were duplicated from originals there. The studio furniture shop constructed a number of replicas of rare pieces, including the dressing table used by Greta Garbo, who played Marguerite Gautier, the tragic heroine of Dumas's classic love story. A quaint old "lover's seat," a form of chaise lounge shaped like the letter S, an inlaid desk, a maple table, and a jewel case inlaid in bronze were among the importations gathered from Europe by Edwin B. Willis.

"One of our odd problems," said Willis, "was in the matter of carpets of the time. Such samples as could be found were so faded that we could hardly trace the weave let alone

(L to R) Gibbons, set visitor Harry Beaumont, George Cukor, and unit art director Fredric Hope on the set of *Camille* in 1936.

the color. We found some notes among the books of a firm centuries old, describing some of the carpets of the period to prospective purchasers, and these gave us accurate data from which we had carpets woven."

Nathalie Bucknall and her indefatigable research department unearthed the actual spot where the "love cottage" depicted in the film was located. Following a lengthy exchange of cables between Hollywood and Paris, Bucknall reported to director George Cukor that extensive research revealed Marguerite and Armand lived in a small house that formerly stood near the Seine River in the province Seine et Oise.

"The cottage," she said, "is 16 kilometers from Versailles where the river makes a U-turn. There, the island of Croissy is situated and the house stood directly opposite the island. The nearest small town is Bougival, mentioned in the story." Director Cukor even asked the research department to determine if the spires of Paris could be seen from the cottage windows in 1847. Research proved they could not.

The Good Earth, Thalberg's filmization of Pearl S. Buck's Pulitzer Prize–winning novel, presented an entirely different set of design and research challenges. Planning on this project was also begun in 1934, when Thalberg first approached actor Paul Muni about playing the lead male character, Chinese farmer Wang Lung. In 1935 Toluboff led a fact-finding mission to China. MGM had engaged the services of General Ting-Hsui Tu, a faculty member at the Central Military Academy in the West Point of China, as a technical advisor and a liaison with the government. With Tu in charge, Toluboff and his associates traveled to farmland mentioned in the story, took hundreds of photographs of scenic vistas, and investigated conditions in several Chinese film studios. Although Thalberg briefly considered making the film in China, he ultimately decided to film the entire story on the backlot.

One of the objectives of the mission, of course, was to collect props and other objects—which ultimately amounted to 380 packing cases. Director Sidney Franklin, whom Thalberg had assigned to direct the film after his first choice, Victor Fleming, was

Above: The village as it appears in *The Good Earth.*

Left: A model of the Chinese village set is perched above the hillside where it will be built.

hospitalized with a kidney infection, described one approach the company used: "A farm would be approached. 'How much for everything?' the farmer would be asked. He'd name his figure. Then a motor lorry would arrive, and workmen would start moving everything movable on the farm. The plows and implements, the cooking utensils in the kitchen, furniture—all went into the lorry, leaving the farmer with more money than he had ever seen in his life."

Faced with constructing acres of terraced Chinese farmland, as well as a Chinese village, Gibbons realized that the backlot would prove inadequate to such an undertaking. A section of California hillside, some five hundred acres in area, was leased near Culver City. Because of the production's size, before filming began Gibbons conceived the idea of creating a scenario of the narrative so that settings, costumes, and camera angles could all be coordinated. Dan Grosbeck, an internationally known illustrator whose drawings for the *Saturday Evening Post* and other publications had earned him a measure of fame, was hired by Gibbons to prepare a series of drawings depicting every bit of action in every scene of the film. Grosbeck was not unknown in Hollywood; he had worked as a concept artist for Cecil B. DeMille in the 1920s. Further, he had traveled extensively in China and had worked with Harry Oliver, one of the unit art directors assigned to the film, on several projects before Oliver came to MGM. When Grosbeck was finished, his drawings were printed and assembled into a book. Oliver, Arnold Gillespie, Edwin Willis, and cameraman Karl Freund each received a copy for their own reference.

Irving Thalberg died on September 14, 1936, when *The Good Earth* was nearing completion. Upon its release early the next year, Mayer inserted a title card after the credits that read, "To the memory of Irving Grant Thalberg, We Dedicate this Picture, His Last Great Achievement." Several productions that Thalberg had been planning but did not live to complete—the aforementioned *Marie Antoinette*, as well as *Goodbye, Mr. Chips* and a film version of Jane Austen's *Pride and Prejudice*—would later go before the cameras. When he was researching the sets for the latter film, which starred Greer Garson

Chinese Street, with the Great Wall in the background.

and Laurence Olivier, Gibbons discovered a complete set of *Ackermann's Repository of Art and Fashion*, forty unique volumes covering every phase of English fashions, furnishings, and architecture from 1809 to 1829. Costume designer Adrian was particularly pleased to find that the magazines contained actual samples of dress materials more than one hundred years old. They had never been touched and were as bright and crisp as the day they were made.

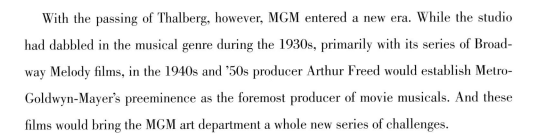

With the passing of Thalberg, however, MGM entered a new era. While the studio had dabbled in the musical genre during the 1930s, primarily with its series of Broad-way Melody films, in the 1940s and '50s producer Arthur Freed would establish Metro-Goldwyn-Mayer's preeminence as the foremost producer of movie musicals. And these films would bring the MGM art department a whole new series of challenges.

CHAPTER EIGHT

THE METRO MUSICALS

THE FIRST PHASE OF WHAT WOULD LATER come to be known as the "MGM musical" had its beginnings in the late summer of 1928. With great fanfare two soundproof stages, the largest to be found at any studio at the time, were "christened" with a ribbon-cutting ceremony attended by most of the studio's executives and many of its contract players. The stages were designed by Verne O. Knudsen, a professor of physics at UCLA. Only months after the stages were opened, Knudsen would become one of the founders of a society that would eventually include up to 450 scientists and engineers interested in the principles of acoustics.

Each stage measured 100 by 125 feet and was surrounded by 8-inch concrete walls with an air gap between the outside and the plaster layer inside. This created a sound-proof vacuum. The floor of each building was 16 inches thick and consisted of concrete, cork, sand, and several layers of timber. When the two-ton doors on each stage were closed, the interiors were hermetically sealed, and ventilation was supplied to each building through sound filters. Six soundproof camera booths housed, in addition to the camera equipment, motors synchronized with the recording instruments.

As Lucy Fischer has noted in her book *Art Direction and Production Design*, these new sound stages would be central to MGM's subsequent industrial dominance. And, as Gibbons soon discovered, they would also change the way art direction was approached at the studio. In these early days, the walls of a set on a stage built for sound could not face each other at right angles, for example, as this would create echoes, while "building sets of proper acoustic material . . . costs about twice as much as building ordinary sets."

The Broadway Melody, Metro-Goldwyn-Mayer's first "all talking, all singing, all dancing" film began shooting on these stages in October 1928 and was released in June of the following year. The film starred Bessie Love and Anita Page as sisters with their own vaudeville act in a backstage story of aspiration, love, and loss. The plot is so stale it was hoary even then, and a few years after its release it was already a museum piece, a victim of, among other things, an evolving improvement in sound recording that liberated the camera from its confining soundproof booth. But even at this very early stage in the development of the movie musical, Irving Thalberg was concerned that one of the big production numbers, "The Wedding of the Painted Doll," looked too stage-bound. "That's not a motion picture," he told his aides after viewing the rushes. "It's not a movie at all; it's a stage presentation. We'll have to do it all over again. This time arrange the cameras, so we can get some different angles, instead of making the audience look at it from the front, as if they were in a legitimate theater." Still, Thalberg wanted to make the film on the cheap, and the entire budget was $350,000. He told his staff, "This is an experiment;

Several exhausted-looking chorus girls take a break on this stage set from *The Broadway Melody.*

we don't know whether the audience will accept a musical on film. So, we'll have to shoot it as fast and cheaply as we can. I want quality, but I don't want to spend a lot of money."

It showed. When Page is set up in a Park Avenue apartment courtesy of a rich playboy, a set from *Our Modern Maidens* was reused to depict the interior. But in 1929 the novelty of sound was enough to make the film one of the biggest hits of the year, with an Academy Award for Best Picture as icing on the cake. MGM followed up with what was essentially a vaudeville show, *The Hollywood Revue of 1929*, in which most of the studio's roster of stars were brought in front of the cameras to sing, dance, or perform comedy routines. Today the film is most famous for introducing the song "Singin' in the Rain," which became a theme song of sorts for the studio. Judy Garland would sing it eleven years later in *Little Nellie Kelly*, and another Kelly would perform his most iconic dance while singing the song in what many consider to be one of the greatest movie musicals ever made.

Cedric Gibbons and Richard Day were responsible for the settings in *Hollywood Revue*, which consisted of little more than scenic backdrops framed by a proscenium arch. Still, whether it was Gibbons or Day who decided to create a background depicting Noah's Ark beached on the side of a mountain while MGM's stars sang their hearts out in the rain, it's visual evidence of a somewhat fiendish sense of humor. And if it was Day's idea, Gibbons still had to approve it.

Other studios also jumped on the musical bandwagon, but by the end of 1930, the trend had passed. Only fourteen musicals were released in 1931, down from one hundred that had premiered the previous year. The market had become oversaturated, the public was losing interest, and films that had originally been conceived as musicals were now cut by their studios to turn them into straight comedies or dramas. Warner Brothers and RKO would both single-handedly revive the genre in 1933 with, respectively, Busby Berkeley's kaleidoscopic choreography and the choreographed courtship of Fred Astaire and Ginger Rogers. And that same year, Thalberg began thinking about making a sound version of Franz Lehár's operetta *The Merry Widow*. MGM had filmed it as a silent in 1925 starring John Gilbert and Mae Murray, with Erich von Stroheim behind the camera. The sound version would star Jeanette MacDonald as the widow, Madame Sonia, and Maurice Chevalier as Count Danilo, her prospective suitor. Looking for a Continental touch, Thalberg engaged Ernst Lubitsch to direct.

The studio marshaled its forces for this slight tale that concerned a rich widow who lives in the tiny (and imaginary) European municipality of Marshovia and its king's attempts to keep the widow and her money in the country by finding the right husband for her. There were forty-four sets. More than five hundred props, hardware, and other fixtures were either rented from antique and decorator shops in the Los Angeles area or imported from Europe to dress them. The set depicting the Marshovian embassy in Paris was the largest set built on a sound stage at MGM up to that time, and it was here that the famous "Merry Widow Waltz" was staged for the cameras, with 180 dancers performing under the tutelage of Albertina Rasch.

Today, the film is almost as well known for two of its most lavish sets as it is for its music and choreography. In 1934 Gibbons was beginning to experiment with livable modern interiors for films set in the present day, but when called upon to create the court of a make-believe middle European kingdom in the late nineteenth century, along with the boudoir of its richest citizen, an agile and unfettered imagination was essential. In designing these sets with unit art director Fredric Hope, Gibbons would again break his own rule—"A movie set should never talk; that should be left to the cast"—with two extraordinary settings that, unlike in *Our Modern Maidens*, worked brilliantly within the context of the film. One would simultaneously broadcast and underscore the loneliness of a rich widow, while the other would playfully draw attention to the farcical dimensions of the plot's central problem.

Fredric Hope had worked alongside Hobe Erwin to create Jean Harlow's all-white boudoir in *Dinner at Eight*. For *The Merry Widow*, Hope and Gibbons used twenty gradations of white to design a grand bedchamber for Madame Sonia, the "richest widow in Europe," with elements of everything from the rococo to Ming Dynasty chinoiserie. After having rebuffed the advances of Danilo early in the film, Sonia enters this vast space with its towering ceiling in a black mourning dress designed by Adrian and sinks in front of her white dressing table, attended to by three servants. The soaring height of the set acts to magnify her isolation, and the color white as used here symbolizes the sterility of her current existence. Not a dollop of color anywhere. Stepping out onto her balcony, MacDonald sings, "The night is romantic/and I am alone. . . ." Trapped in MGM's version of an ivory tower.

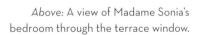

Above: A view of Madame Sonia's bedroom through the terrace window.

Right: Jeanette MacDonald as Madame Sonia, the "richest widow in Europe," sequestered in her all-white bedroom in black mourning dress.

Plotting escape, Madame Sonia soon decamps to Paris, which elicits headlines in Marshovia's only newspaper, *The Morning Moo* ("a paper for stable and table"): "Richest Widow Leaves Country! King Achmed Summons Cabinet." As the scene shifts to Achmed's royal palace, Gibbons summons up memories of his most outlandish Ruritanian fantasies in films such as *Three Weeks*. Only this time, the set is overlaid with so much gilt, and so many oversized emblems of royalty, that it calls out the ludicrousness of a self-important sovereign who rules a country of shepherds at the benevolence of a single subject. In our first glimpse of the set, an overdressed, pompous messenger arrives to deliver the king's royal suspenders.

The outlandish sets depicting King Achmed's palace in *The Merry Widow* underscored the ludicrousness of a self-important sovereign who ruled a tiny country at the benevolence of a single subject.

Director Ernst Lubitsch enjoys tea with actress Una Merkel on the set of *The Merry Widow,* under one of Gibbons's subtle emblems of Marshovian royalty.

The extravagant sets for *The Merry Widow* would establish a design strategy that MGM would follow for a series of musicals that closed out the 1930s. It was during this period that Gibbons began referring to his division as the "architecture and engineering department," and with good reason. When your studio had the largest sound stage in the world, why not use it to full advantage and build a set that reaches God's eyes? It was fully on display in *The Great Ziegfeld* (1936), Thalberg's three-hour biopic of the legendary theatrical producer. To close out the first half of the film, Gibbons and his associates Merrill Pye and John Harkrider designed a plan to stage a production number, ostensibly as part of a Ziegfeld Follies revue within the film, built around Irving Berlin's tune "A Pretty Girl is Like a Melody." Eddie Cantor actually introduced this song to audiences in the *Ziegfeld Follies of 1919*.

Director Robert Z. Leonard, directly behind the camera, prepares a take for the "A Pretty Girl is Like a Melody" number in *The Great Ziegfeld* in front of the enormous volute designed by Gibbons, Pye, and Harkrider.

Thalberg hired Harkrider because he had actually worked with Ziegfeld on several of his stage revues. But he ultimately clashed with Gibbons by insisting, "Ziegfeld wouldn't have done that," to which Gibbons would reply, "Ziegfeld never made a movie." Nevertheless, the trio came up with a design (115 possibilities were submitted in the space of eight days) for a massive spiral volute of structural steel that weighed 100 tons. It was constructed inside Stage 6 on a revolving platform 70 feet in diameter with 75 steps that led up to the apex. A steel ring above the stage carried two curtains made out of 4,300 yards of silk and rayon that was attached to 48 trip lines geared to a reduction transmission. Finally, the cyclorama that surrounded the set stood 80 feet high and was 300 feet in length, with a night sky composed of more than 6,000 blinking lights depicting the Milky Way.

The number opens with Dennis Morgan plaintively singing Berlin's ballad. As he finishes the first chorus, an immense curtain rises gradually to the left, and then stops as the spiral slowly appears and begins to turn, revealing an eighteenth-century tableau lit by candles. Berlin's song then becomes the fulcrum of a series of crescendos that will ultimately include a mixture of Strauss, Verdi, and Gershwin. At first the camera remains stationary, allowing this shimmering scene, in shades of silver and white, to revolve before it. And then midway into the number a second curtain begins to rise, this time straight up, revealing a series of steps. Pianists playing "Rhapsody in Blue" on grand pianos are lined up to the right, and a series of men in formal evening dress stand at attention on the left. The pace picks up, the camera begins to move in an upward trajectory, and the curtain continues to rise, taking us on a trip to the summit of a mount. A series of chorus girls dressed by Adrian in silver masks and black- and silver-sequined body stockings move alternately up and down the staircase as Gershwin thunders on the soundtrack. Not until the camera uncovers actress Virginia Bruce sitting daintily at the top of this creamy revolving column does it begin to pull back, revealing the entire set as the curtain slowly falls and shields it from view.

Two views of the summit, with actress
Virginia Bruce sitting daintily at the top.

The Great Ziegfeld has been criticized, and perhaps justly so, for being stodgy, over-blown, and overlong at a little more than three hours. And four years after Busby Berkeley and his camera had begun leaping across the sound stages at Warner Brothers, some of the film's often static tableaux, by contrast, can seem uninspired. But if Thalberg had managed to borrow Berkeley from Warner's (Berkeley did work for MGM on several films in the early 1940s), MGM would most likely have been accused of imitating another studio's innovative success. Instead it relied on using its art and costume departments to

This set from *The Great Ziegfeld* was designed for a dance number built around the Gregory May song, "You Gotta Pull Strings." It typifies the kind of glamorous, lavish, and yet pristine set that has become inextricably linked to the Gibbons legacy.

best advantage, exploiting the kind of budget few other studios could afford and creating an approximation of the visual astonishment Ziegfeld must have achieved on the stage in his heyday—if he'd had the money and a proscenium arch that touched the clouds. The "Pretty Girl" production number cost two hundred thousand dollars and lasted for nine minutes on the screen. Until the very end of it, the audience was teased into wondering what the set might turn out to be, just how vast it was, and how high it would go, and this is its genius. Over eighty years after it was filmed, it still elicits gasps from an audience.

In its review of the film, the critic for *Variety* described the "Pretty Girl" number as "a scenic flash which makes the auditor wonder 'What can they do to follow that?' meaning in this or future film production." Throughout the rest of the decade, MGM would keep trying to follow it—and top it—though it would never quite succeed. Nothing could ever match that final surprise. The title and backstage spirit of the first *Broadway Melody* would be revived and vivified in a series of films titled after the year of their release: *Broadway Melody of 1936*, *Broadway Melody of 1938*, and *Broadway Melody of 1940*. Eleanor Powell, a tap dancer extraordinaire from vaudeville and Broadway who was signed to an MGM contract in 1935, would appear in all three Broadway Melody revivals, as well as such big budget MGM musicals as *Born to Dance* (1936), *Rosalie* (1937), and *Lady Be Good* (1941).

Since Powell did her own choreography, she consulted closely with the art director assigned to each film. "You would get with the art director and you would say, 'I'd like a fountain and a staircase,' she told John Kobal in 1971. He'd sketch something vaguely to fit with my idea. Because I was going to use that for an effect. You didn't actually design the set, but you gave an idea of what you wanted."

MGM publicity would still breathlessly compare the sets in these films to those constructed for *The Great Ziegfeld*: "There are seven sets, one for each of the songs written for *Born to Dance*. The smallest of the sets covers an entire soundstage while the largest is more than 25 feet higher and 15 feet wider than the 'Pretty Girl' set in *The Great*

Ziegfeld. This set, featuring the 'Swinging the Jinx Away' number, is made of crystal glass and silver, which is high spotted by a huge backdrop covered with 10,000 stars, or 1,000 more than can be viewed at any observatory." The set itself, designed by Gibbons and Pye, represented a battleship built as a modernistic fantasy. Weighing more than 120 tons, it required a 24-hour shift of workmen two months to complete. At the end of the song, the chorus exhorts the camera to go "higher, higher, higher" up a circular stair representing a crow's nest until it reveals Powell, resplendent in a sequined cape, standing against a background of stars. This setting would be a recurring motif that Gibbons would frequently employ, perhaps to suggest that these sets were, indeed, a glimpse of heaven.

The battleship set designed by Gibbons and Pye for *Born to Dance* featured a spiral staircase that, once again, reached for the stars.

Director Roy Del Ruth readies a take on the battleship set for *Born to Dance* against MGM's panorama of stars. Eleanor Powell can be seen, just barely, at the top of the cylindrical staircase.

Eleanor Powell "Swinging the Jinx Away" in *Born to Dance*.

The set for the title number in *Rosalie* was so large it had to be built on vacant land just outside the studio's backlot. No sound stage could contain it.

The stars returned to the heavens in the set for the midfilm climax in *Rosalie* (1937), again starring Powell, this time paired with Nelson Eddy. The trailer for the film showed ten images of the MGM trademark, Leo the Lion, roaring "louder than ever" because he has "ten times more to roar about." Touted as the "thrilling climax of MGM's musical parade," the film was billed as featuring the biggest movie set since *Ben-Hur*. Not even one of MGM's massive sound stages could contain it, and it was built on sixty acres of

Nelson Eddy and Eleanor Powell tie the knot in a simple wedding ceremony as conceived by MGM's art department.

vacant land just beyond the backlot. Nine cameras were used to film the sequence, in which Eleanor Powell dances down a curved series of drums that grow smaller as she descends. The ninth camera was manned by director W. S. Van Dyke II. It was attached to the end of a ninety-foot boom that in turn was part of an eight-wheeled platform. His camera never quit moving, for as the boom moved up and down, the platform moved with it.

For *Broadway Melody of 1938*, curtains were once again emphasized. The world's "largest and heaviest" curtain, composed of solid, unbreakable glass, appeared in the finale. Controlled by hydraulic pressure, it was lowered backward to the floor of the stage to become a series of steps on which Powell, George Murphy, and one hundred other dancers performed a waltz step. Once the curtain fell, the "Broadway" set was revealed. Twelve modernistic buildings, from one to eight stories in height, were raised by means of ten thousand pounds of pressure. A series of cabs, trucks, and cars made their way around the set, operated by a man sitting at an electrical switchboard.

The following year, 1939, the ripple of a sea change occurred in the evolution of the MGM musical. Arthur Freed had been writing songs for the studio since he was hired as a songwriter at $250 a week in 1929 and, along with his partner, Nacio Herb Brown, he wrote the songs for the original *Broadway Melody* and several for *The Hollywood Revue*, including "You Were Meant for Me," "Singin' in the Rain," "All I Do Is Dream of You," "You Are My Lucky Star," and "Broadway Rhythm." After working—uncredited—as an associate producer on *The Wizard of Oz*, Freed, a Louis B. Mayer favorite, was given his own production unit within the company. More than any other person in the studio hierarchy, it was Freed who would nurture and promote what millions of people around the world came to recognize as the "MGM musical" in the 1940s and '50s.

More has been written about the filming of *The Wizard of Oz* than perhaps any other American film, with the possible exceptions of *Citizen Kane* and *Gone with the Wind*. The film was a Herculean effort on the part of the art department. More than sixty-five sets were designed and constructed. As with *Romeo and Juliet* and other epic MGM

A lavish set for the finale of *Broadway Melody of 1938*.

productions, each design was made into a model from blueprints and color schemes planned out long in advance. Munchkinland, built on Stage 30, stood ninety feet high and contained twenty-two tiny houses, giant flowers, a public square, a bridge over a tiny river, a fountain, marketplaces, and streets. The field of red poppies where Dorothy and the Cowardly Lion fell asleep covered an acre and a half, and twenty men worked for a solid week sticking the two-foot wire stems into the set.

While Adrian could obtain inspiration for the costumes from L. Frank Baum's sometimes lengthy descriptions of each character's appearance down to the apparel they wore, William Horning, the unit art director Gibbons assigned to the film, discovered there were no descriptions or illustrations in the many editions of the book that could assist the art department in visualizing the world of Oz. And while there was a Munchkin country referred to in the original story, there was no mention, let alone a description, of a specific Munchkin town or city. Jack Martin Smith, who was a sketch artist at MGM at the time and would later go on to become a unit art director before becoming head of the art department at 20th Century Fox in 1956, was assigned by Gibbons to turn Horning's initial ideas into thumbnails. "Ordinarily," said Smith, "you could go to a book or a town and say, 'I'm going to do this type of architecture.' For *Meet Me in St. Louis* (1944) I had oil paintings, steel engravings, and carpentry books. So, I could more or less copy a house that would have been there, in St. Louis, in 1900. But all Oz had to be imagined and created."

Once the thumbnails met with the approval of both Gibbons and Horning, Smith was assigned to make much larger sketches in full color. But when he saw the sketches, Gibbons rejected them, although it was not a reflection on Smith's ability. He had decided that since Oz was, literally, a dream world, the color should be more subdued. In 1939 everyone was nervous about using three-strip technicolor; the first film using the process, *Becky Sharp*, had been released only three years before. There were, in fact, "color advisors" from the Technicolor company on every MGM film shot in color until after World War II.

And then there was the problem of creating the audience's first look at the Emerald City after Dorothy and the Lion wake up in the poppy field sprinkled with snow. Both Gibbons and Horning rejected sketch after sketch as too ridiculously baroque or too conventionally (and recognizably) moderne. It was Gibbons who eventually solved the problem. Apart from the massive library—both books and clipping files—that the research department had amassed since the early 1930s, Gibbons had his own personal library of books and magazines on aspects of architecture and interior design as well as painting and sculpture. Burrowing though this collection for days, he finally unearthed what he

Above: Jack Martin Smith's second depiction of the Emerald City featured more subdued colors, and he carpeted the interior with the red poppies that surrounded the approach to the city.

Left: Munchkinland in *The Wizard of Oz,* as conceptualized by unit art director Jack Martin Smith.

Munchkinland was built within the vast confines of MGM's Stage 30

was looking for. "He found a tiny, really miniscule photograph of a sketch that had been done in Germany pre–World War I," says Smith. "We looked at the sketch—it actually looked like test tubes upside down—and it crystallized our ideas." The first glimpse of the exterior of the Emerald City, as well as the witch's castle, would be created as matte paintings—a color painting on a four-foot-wide piece of black cardboard. The aerial view of the witch's castle silhouetted against the sky was another matte painting.

Several months after *The Wizard of Oz* went into wide release in the autumn of 1939, Freed made one of his first major decisions as head of his own production unit when he hired a designer from New York and brought him to MGM. Vincente Minnelli had been working as a set designer in New York since the early 1930s, following a stint in Chicago where he designed costumes and sets for the Balaban and Katz theater chain. He had worked as a set designer at Radio City Music Hall shortly after the theater opened in 1932, and by 1935 he was directing and staging shows for the Shuberts and Florenz Ziegfeld. Minnelli was initially hired by Freed to work as a "consultant," particularly on musical numbers, but both men knew that Minnelli's primary ambition in coming to MGM was to ultimately make his own films.

When he learned about Minnelli, Gibbons immediately fired off a memo to MGM's comptroller and general manager, Eddie Mannix:

> For your information we have signed Vincent Manelli [sic], a New York stage designer. This was done through Arthur Freed. In speaking to Arthur on Saturday he told me about this man and he said he was engaged as a dance director. I said, "Nothing else?" And he said, "for ideas on dance numbers and musical settings, etc." I am afraid Eddie that this will be another Harkrider-Hobe-Irwin-[sic]-Oliver Messel situation and if you remember you and I chatted at great length about this type of thing some time ago—and I want to reiterate that I absolutely refuse to work under any conditions with any man designing settings unless he is brought through to me as a member of my department. This man may be the world's greatest genius. If he is, by all means give him my job. I find it tough enough as it is to work with the most sympathetic assistants I can secure. I do not feel that any of my men should take orders from anyone other than myself in the matter of set design, whether it be for musical numbers or the interiors of submarines. Do you think we need further experience in these expensive experiments? Not just the man's salary, but what he actually costs us. I, for one, had thought we had learned our lesson. Gibby.

For his part Minnelli, in his early dealings with the MGM art department, would refer to it as a "medieval fiefdom, its overlord accustomed to doing things in a certain way . . . his own." In an interview conducted in the late 1960s, he elaborated. "I had problems with the MGM art department; I had to revolutionize them initially. They were shocked at a lot of the things I wanted to do. At the beginning it was rather a strain, but they saw everything my way in the end."

Gibbons could sometimes be intransigent about procedure, but this didn't mean he wasn't open to new ideas. The initial problem between the two was a failing on the part of both men to recognize or appreciate the other's unique experience. While Minnelli had a refined and often unerring visual sense, honed by years of work on the stage, he had virtually no knowledge of architecture and would sometimes insist on something that would be impossible to photograph. He also had a laissez-faire attitude toward budgets. Keogh Gleason, a set decorator at MGM who worked under Edwin Willis, recalled that "I was always being called on the carpet, because Minnelli was asking for the moon on a silver platter. He'd say, 'we'll have this,' and I'd say, 'Yes, we can do it, but it's going to be expensive.' Then he'd say, 'Well, let's not bother about the cost.' So there'd be J. J. Cohn, who'd tell me, 'God, don't give him everything he wants, only the essentials.'"

Communication, however, was the main impediment. "Vincente Minnelli is a very unique individual," said Preston Ames, "very difficult to work with, because his lack of communication is unbelievable. And then, on the other hand, he knows what he wants, and sometimes you can figure out what he wants, sometimes you can't." Gleason noted that "when communicating with Minnelli, it's like he tells you the second paragraph before he tells you the first." And George Gibson, head of the scenic art department in the 1940s and 1950s, remembered one conference that took place before *Brigadoon* began production in 1954:

> Cedric Gibbons had an idea of doing it one way, but it didn't sit too well with Minnelli, who wanted it another way. So, Cedric Gibbons

Vincente Minnelli and Cedric Gibbons on the set of an unnamed film in the late 1940s. Antagonistic at first, they learned to respect each other's unique talents.

said, "We'll get a hold of Gibson and Ames, and let's talk it over." So, with myself and Preston Ames and Cedric Gibbons in his office, Minnelli outlined all of what he was thinking about. This was grasping at straws; you had to be something of a mind reader to know what Minnelli wanted. After Minnelli left, Cedric Gibbons looked at Ames, and he looked at me, and he said, "Mr. Ames and Mr. Gibson, you may know what has been discussed here, but I don't!" And we didn't either, if you want to know the truth; we didn't either."

Andrew Sarris, a leading proponent of the auteur theory in film criticism, once wrote that "Minnelli believed more in beauty than in art." Minnelli unknowingly corroborated this idea when he was in Argentina for a film festival in the early 1960s. He told interviewers for *Movie* magazine that "the visual aspect has always been important to me because of the way you place actors in time, in space, and in their environment . . . each time the kind of story that you're using has to dictate a certain visual feeling. I try to find the style that belongs to that particular film, not to any other film. Now, within that frame, I work with the art directors, because I've been an art director myself. I do a great deal of research and try to find the style and color sense for that particular film."

The first major clash that took place between Minnelli and the MGM art department came during preproduction planning on *Meet Me in St. Louis*, the now-classic musical based on a series of short stories by Sally Benson, and originally published in the *New Yorker* under the title "5135 Kensington." World War II was raging overseas, and Gibbons, mindful of the restraints that the war had placed on all the major studios, wanted to redress "Andy Hardy Street" on the backlot to resemble turn-of-the-century St. Louis. In August 1942 the *New York Times* reported that "scarcely a branch of film production remains unaffected by war freezes . . . inroads into personnel have been great and will become greater. . . . Metals, lumber, paints and burlap; fiber-board, wallpaper, muslin, and dress materials; rope, makeup, electric wiring and lamps; even the raw material of the movies—the film itself—are not to be had or are budgeted in their purpose and use." But Minnelli was obstinate, and Freed went to see Mayer, who was already invested in the story. Freed told him, "I want to make this into the most delightful piece of Americana ever . . . it'll cost a bit, but it'll be great." Although Mayer looked apprehensive, he gave Freed the go-ahead, and an actual street of turn-of-the-century Victorian homes began to rise on the lot. Redressing the Andy Hardy street would have cost a little less than sixty thousand dollars. The new "St. Louis Street," as people at the studio would later refer to it, would cost more than two hundred thousand dollars to build. But MGM eventually made money off of the extensive set, renting it out to other film companies and TV shows well into the 1960s.

To assist in designing the film, Freed and Minnelli brought Broadway stage designer Lemuel Ayers to MGM. Ayers had designed *The Pirate*, with Lunt and Fontanne, in 1942 and the original production of *Oklahoma!* the following year. As was becoming standard with imported talent, Gibbons appointed Jack Martin Smith to oversee Ayers's work, and of course every sketch and idea had to be approved by Gibbons and Minnelli. Edwin Willis scoured the property department for props, and the buying sprees the studio had embarked on in the 1930s proved fruitful, allowing him to make his own unique contributions. Grandpa's bureau in the film, for example, is cluttered with a wide variety of strange and peculiar hats, bearing witness to the character's age and eccentricities. "The décor of *Meet Me in St. Louis* is not a realistic representation but a memory," film historian Joseph

"St. Louis Street" was built on the MGM backlot at Minnelli's insistence.

Above; The wraparound porch and front door of the Smith home on St. Louis Street.

Right: The entrance to the Smith home was chockablock with authentic furnishings from the turn of the nineteenth century.

Andrew Casper has written. "A happy reflection, the film's décor is idealized and tinged with a shade of pathos and is consequently psychologically and dramatically accurate."

As a follow-up, Freed veered from the sentimental to the colossal, with one of the last of MGM's big Ziegfeld-inspired productions. He may have been encouraged by the relaxation of war restrictions on construction materials early in 1945. *Ziegfeld Follies* (1946) was a revue without a connecting plot, and Minnelli was responsible for five segments: "This Heart of Mine," "Limehouse Blues," "A Great Lady Has an Interview," "The Babbitt and the Bromide," and "There's Beauty Everywhere." It was the last number that signaled the death knell for this type of musical, at least at MGM.

Grandfather Smith's room in *Meet Me in St. Louis* featured a collection of hats from different periods and cultures, bearing witness to the character's age and eccentricities.

Vincente Minnelli (center, left) rehearses Judy Garland and Tom Drake on the set, still under construction, that will represent the Louisiana Purchase Exposition at the end of *Meet Me in St. Louis*.

"There's Beauty Everywhere" was conceived as the finale of the film, with Fred Astaire, Lucille Bremer, and Cyd Charisse dancing to singer James Melton's rendition of the title tune, written by Freed himself with Harry Warren. Instead of using dissolves, choreographer Robert Alton came up with the idea of using a bubble machine to make the finale "an iridescent, shimmering, supernatural kaleidoscope of color." As Randall

Duell remembers, "I had Astaire dancing through bubbles that were ten feet deep, and he put up with it. It was difficult to do choreography because of those bubbles, which was aerosol with hot water. . . . Astaire ruined several tuxedos, and the pants were wet, and he had to change them all the time."

Then disaster struck. During one take the machine malfunctioned, sending aerosol bubbles into the hallways of the sound stage. They "poured out like lava from a volcano and the fire brigade was called. Bubbles streamed down the sides, into caves, into every crevice. Armed with oversized badminton rackets, several grips were detailed to keep the bubbles in place. They went around swatting unruly ones." Minnelli later said, "You've

Although obviously staged for publicity purposes, this still from the production number "There's Beauty Everywhere" may represent the exact moment when Vincente Minnelli realized that "you can't direct soap bubbles."

got to remember, you can't direct bubbles!" And Gibbons, whose sense of humor is rarely remarked upon, said, "Mr. Duell, if that set wasn't big and white before, it certainly will be now."

The number as it was originally conceived was eliminated from the film. Not long afterward, just before the film's release, Duell said Freed told him privately that it was time to bring the musical back to the audience: "Let's bring it back to earth," he said. "Let's do away with the era of opulence." Duell later stated, "The audience became glutted about 1943, I think, with films like *Ziegfeld Follies*. We oversaturated with whipped cream." And bubbles.

Yet the "era of opulence" celebrated in *Ziegfeld Follies* produced one final masterpiece of design and choreography in Minnelli's "Limehouse Blues." It was devised as a dramatic pantomime, set in London's "Limehouse" district, with Fred Astaire as a poverty-stricken Chinese man who becomes infatuated with a beautiful Chinese woman, played by Lucille Bremer. Jack Martin Smith made expert use of the waterfront set, still standing, that had been constructed the previous year for *The Picture of Dorian Gray*, revising and painting it in monotones of beige, grey, brown, and black and pumping in "London fog" to help set the mood. Minnelli conceived the atmosphere for the rest of the set; the background characters materialize before the camera in a long tracking shot: a sailor staring out over a dock, streetwalkers plying their trade, a drunken woman looking for handouts, a man with a phonograph in a baby carriage strolling the streets, and several "costermongers" who were well-known street singers and dancers in the Limehouse district. For the fantasy dance sequence, the set was a riot of French chinoiserie, with bridges, pagodas, pavilions, and Astaire and Bremer weaving and whirling in radiating red costumes holding candy apple–colored fans against a background bathed in cobalt-blue light.

In the decade that followed the release of *Ziegfeld Follies* in 1946, Freed would, for the most part, bring the MGM musical "back to Earth." Budget constraints, due to falling

Above: An almost Daliesque riot of chinoiserie surrounds Fred Astaire and Lucille Bremer.

Left: The opening shots of the "Limehouse Blues" number from *Ziegfeld Follies* used the atmospheric waterfront set that had been constructed the previous year for *The Picture of Dorian Gray.*

profits with the arrival of television and the Southern Federal District Court edict that the major studios had to divest themselves of their theater chains, were also a factor. Preston Ames, Jack Martin Smith, and Randall Duell have all commented on how these developments affected their duties in the art department. "In those days," said Ames, "we spent every nickel we could scrounge to make the most presentable setting that you could." Duell remembers, "Often times, Gene [Kelly] didn't have the budget to do what he wanted to do, and he put a lot of faith in me that I would come up with something without [spending] a lot of money."

Despite these restrictions, directors such as Minnelli, Charles Walters, and the team of Stanley Donen and Gene Kelly would continue to make some of MGM's greatest musicals: *The Pirate* (1948), *Easter Parade* (1948), *On the Town* (1949), *An American in Paris* (1951), *Singin' in the Rain* (1952), *The Band Wagon* (1953), and *Seven Brides for Seven Brothers* (1954), to name a few. Many of them became classics precisely because they showcased the musical talent on view rather than the production values. Minnelli's *The Pirate* starred Judy Garland and Gene Kelly and was based on a play by S. N. Behrman. Set in the imaginary town of Calvados in the Caribbean, Garland plays Manuela, a young woman who is engaged to the town's wealthy mayor. But she has romantic dreams of being carried off by a legendary pirate named Macoco, also known as "Mack the Black." Kelly plays a traveling player who falls in love with Manuela and impersonates Macoco to try to impress her. At first, Minnelli considered using actual locations, but this was still frowned upon. In any case, he soon decided he wanted to stress stylization and give the film a decidedly artificial flavor.

The studio was still experimenting with technicolor at this time, and Minnelli wanted bright, vivid colors for Calvados. The unit art director, Jack Martin Smith, understood: "When you talk about the Caribbean you're talking about bright blues, azures, and then all the warm colors, the oranges, the corals, the reds, the whites. It's not as if you're up in Maine and just showing the grey house and the beautiful knotty tree beside it, and a piece

The balcony of Manuela's (Judy Garland) bedroom in *The Pirate*. Note the decrepit, almost crumbling stone of the balcony that indicates the age of the Caribbean village where the story takes place.

of grey-blue water. You're down in the Caribbean, so you want to see really go-to-town colors." This necessitated a great deal of preproduction work in order to avoid colors that would clash. For one thing, Smith would have to coordinate the colors on the set with the costumes each actor wore, and he worked closely with MGM costume supervisor Irene. Gibbons had hired three people from Technicolor to cut swatches, and color samples were placed on cards that indicated what color the walls would be painted as well as the colors for all the costumes. Smith would make large color drawings of the exterior and interior sets and present them to the "Technicolor advisor" to see if the color scheme would be suitable.

The technicolor musicals starring Esther Williams presented a different set of problems, because many of the production numbers were shot underwater. A piece of canvas would be painted with the color the art director wanted to use. It would then be submerged in the water to see how it would photograph at ten, twenty, or thirty feet away from the camera. In many cases, the results were startling. Bright orange, for example, tended to go gray when shot from a distance of twenty feet.

The major film studios could not purchase technicolor cameras; they could only rent them from the Technicolor company that had invented the three-strip process. The camera's major drawback in the 1940s was the fact that it required a large, unwieldy sound blimp. When Kelly and Donen were planning their first directorial effort, a film version of Comden and Green's *On the Town*, they wanted to shoot the entire film in New York. But due to budget constraints and the still cumbersome cameras, this was impossible. It was ultimately decided that a single unit would go to New York to shoot exterior scenes with the six principals—Gene Kelly, Frank Sinatra, Jules Munshin, Betty Garrett, Ann Miller, and Vera-Ellen—while Jack Martin Smith worked on the interiors at MGM. Smith found his most challenging assignment to be a re-creation of the Empire State Building roof at midnight, with the lights of the city beyond it. He placed a mock-up of the roof in the Esther Williams swimming pool on Stage 30, making an island that rose forty-five feet in the air. Behind it was a 250-foot-wide backdrop with the New York skyline rendered in tempera. Smith painstakingly cut out tiny windows and placed lights behind them. Placing the mock-up in the pool allowed the camera to shoot upward when Munshin was hanging over the ledge of the roof.

The desire to break the bonds of the sound stage and film in actual, real-world locations would become a contentious issue in the 1950s. While preparing *The Band Wagon* in 1953, Ames took Vincente Minnelli to a street carnival that was taking place in Santa Monica that had, as Ames described it, "a real 'carny' kind of a look to it." The purpose for the trip was to get ideas for the penny arcade setting in the film, where Fred Astaire sings "A Shine on Your Shoes." As Ames recalled, "Minnelli and I walked it for hours to see what there was, what happened, what people did, what people around it did, so that he kind of saw this before he ever saw a stage set. In other words, he realized the potential of the fortune teller and of the gimmick that exploded and the slot machine and all the other stuff." Minnelli was so enthused he wanted to film the sequence on location

at the carnival until Freed dissuaded him. But the eagerness to get beyond the confines of the sound stage would continue to grow, not just on Minnelli's part but for Kelly and Donen also.

For *The Band Wagon* Freed imported Broadway designer Oliver Smith to work with the art department, ostensibly because many of the numbers in the film would be executed on a stage, and for once Gibbons took no offense. Most likely this was because Gibbons was Smith's idol. "He's one of the reasons I went into scenic design," Smith said, "going to movies and seeing Gibbons's scenery and productions, which were enormously stylish." Smith's contract stipulated that his services would include serving as a

Leroy Daniels gives Fred Astaire a shine on his shoes in an amusement arcade inspired by a street carnival in Santa Monica.

consultant in the preparation and production of *The Band Wagon* and as required would serve as art director, designer, writer, choreographer, librettist, and codirector of ballet. This all-encompassing list of possible responsibilities was typical when the studio engaged a freelance designer for one assignment, as the producers didn't know exactly how his or her talents would be used until the production was underway.

The rest of the art department was wary of this "intruder" in their ranks. Ames said, "Oliver took a look at me and I took a look at him and I thought, 'How are we going to get along?'" Not well, as it turned out. Smith later recalled that when they were doing the interiors the two men would use whatever they could find in the warehouse and then revamp it, but that it was Smith who made the final decision. This eventually gave rise to a tremendous row when both Smith and Minnelli wanted to use a bottle-green backdrop with a vivid red sofa in front of it in the "Girl Hunt Ballet" number. Gibbons always felt that the combination of red and green would remind everyone in the audience of Christmas. (Minnelli once retorted, when he and Gibbons were working on *Meet Me in St. Louis*, that God must have made a terrible mistake when he designed red roses.) Gibbons eventually gave in. He was only three years away from retirement in 1953, and perhaps he felt these kinds of battles were really not worth waging anymore.

Singin' in the Rain had no need for location shooting, as the majority of the film was set in a Hollywood studio during the 1920s. Gene Kelly wanted to shoot the "You Were Meant for Me" number in an empty sound stage on the lot. He and Randall Duell walked around one day until they found a sound stage that had nothing in it but a ladder and a string of lights. Kelly walked over to the ladder and placed his hands on it. "This is great," he told Duell. "The studio at that time had a fantastic backlog of what we call units, stock units," said Duell. "We would take units from some other picture and use some of the basic units and redesign them to fit our set. It saved us a lot of money to be able to use some door units and window units and things of that nature. Or if there was a big staircase or something where we could just change a rail, we would

A New York street, constructed on the backlot in the mid-1930s, was the setting for Gene Kelly's iconic "Singin' in the Rain" number. The planks indicate where arrows will eventually be drawn to show where Kelly has to hit his marks during the filming.

use it." Another stroll around the lot would provide the setting for the title number. As Duell recalls,

> They didn't want to spend a lot of money building a set on a stage. Gene said, "Maybe we can do it on the street." So, we went out to one of the little streets and finally picked a street where we thought it might work out. Gene said, "Let's try to lay it out on this street." They took a piano out onto the street with a tempo track, just for the beat of the music, and began to work with that, and Gene began to work out his number. Then we laid out every step. For instance, when he would jump off a box or down on the pavement or something, he had

to land in a puddle. We would draw a circle where that puddle was to be built. We would rearrange the architecture of the thing to accommodate the exact split second when he was there to test whatever it was. Then we would dish out the street and repave it and make all these puddles so that he hit exactly where he was going to go. When the company went out to shoot it, the street was wet down, and it was raining, and everything was lovely. It took several weeks of working with Gene to get the puddles right.

Brigadoon and *Seven Brides for Seven Brothers*, among the last musicals Gibbons worked on before he retired, tested the veracity of sound stage sets as opposed to location shooting. These films were also made after the introduction of CinemaScope, which affected the construction of sets, because they had to be made to extreme proportions in order to accommodate the wide screen. In *Brigadoon* Americans Tommy Albright (Gene Kelly) and Jeff Douglas (Van Johnson) discover a quaint and beautiful village in the highlands of Scotland while on a vacation only to discover that it appears for only one day every one hundred years. The trick was re-creating those highlands on a sound stage. "The whole thing was a stage set," Preston Ames recalled years later:

> We never went outdoors once. We had two stage sets on one stage and, of course, in those days Metro had some pretty fabulous stages. Our Stage 27 was 75 feet high, about 250 feet long, and about 150 feet deep, which is a pretty good-sized stage. I had a piece of set on one end of the stage, and I had another piece of set on the other end of the stage, and I looked at it one day very, very carefully, and I went back to my boss, Cedric Gibbons, and I said, "Mr. Gibbons, I have a horrible idea." "What is it?" "I'd like to put those two sets together." And he said, "What did you have in mind?" And I said, "This thing calls for sheep and little running streams and all this other jazz, and I feel I can make it. It's going to cost a little money, but I feel I can make a tremendous thing." So, he said, "Let's take the director down [to the

Cyd Charisse, Gene Kelly, and Gibbons inspect a set model for *Brigadoon*.

The atmospheric set for *Brigadoon* created by unit art director Preston Ames.

set]." Minnelli isn't one to go overboard on appreciation, because he feels that this is part of your job, and he couldn't believe that all of a sudden out of two things came one tremendous thing. It turned out to be very successful.

The "tremendous thing" turned out to be the central set of the village itself, and the background vistas that surrounded it. When Ames was finished, everywhere Minnelli turned the camera it showed a different vista.

Stanley Donen later expressed regret, after *Seven Brides for Seven Brothers* had finished shooting, that MGM hadn't allow him to film on location. But without controlled lighting and the installation of flooring that could be maintained in take after take during the dance sequences, location shooting became problematic. "There is a certain thinking today that no film should ever be made except outside the walls of the studio," Ames said in 1973. "In certain cases, great, I couldn't believe it more. In other instances, it's ridiculous. And, strangely enough, you'll find that a director who insists on going outdoors or going to a location, and doing everything for real, suddenly finds that someone will say to him, "Mr. Director, if we had this on a stage, we'd be able to pull out some of these walls, and you could get some of these shots." All of a sudden they have discovered a studio, and they think that this is pretty great stuff."

With the filming of what many consider to be the "quintessential MGM musical," *An American in Paris*, in 1951, many of these issues came to a head. The way they were confronted and resolved opens a window onto just how instrumental the art department was to the creation not only of the MGM musicals but to every film MGM made.

The idea behind *An American in Paris* was born, so to speak, with Freed's desire to build a movie around the Gershwins' song catalog. Long before the film went into production, Gibbons assigned Preston Ames to the film as the unit art director. Ames had never worked with Minnelli before, but he had lived in Paris for five years as an architecture student. "He [Gibbons] felt," said Ames, "and rightly so, that I would be very much at home with this picture." In addition, there were two or three art directors on staff who refused to work with Minnelli because he was famous for throwing out sets at the last minute. Edwin Willis was one man in the art department who went out of his way not to have any direct dealings with Minnelli.

Keogh Gleason remembers the day he was called into Willis's office, and Willis told him it was his turn for the "kiss of fire." Gleason had to dress the sets for *Father of the Bride* (1950), in which Spencer Tracy plays a middle-aged, middle-class father who, with his wife, is planning a wedding for his only daughter. "Well," said Gleason, "Minnelli says to me, 'Of course, at the reception, all will be silver.' I said, 'You mean the gifts.' And he said, 'Oh, no, at the reception, before the gifts.' I said, 'Where does he get silver on $25,000 a year?' He says, 'They borrowed it from the neighbors.' Well, I decorated the house set, and Minnelli walks in with his entourage, and nobody says a word. Finally, he said, 'Keogh, it's perfect.' After that, Ed Willis said, 'Keogh, you're it!'" And that's how Gleason was assigned to *An American in Paris*.

Gibbons worked very closely with Ames to break down the script into scenes and make decisions on what they were going to need to build, what stages they would need, and what could be used on the backlot. Walter Strohm, the production manager on *An American in Paris*, remembers that "in the meetings, Gibbons would sit there and read scenes and discuss the acting. It was a general open meeting about a picture. There were no restraints put on people as to what they could or could not talk about. Gibbons would say what he thought at any given time, Freed said what he thought about Gibbons's idea, and I could say what I thought about both of their ideas. Now, we had arguments; don't think they were all tea parties. It couldn't be any other way with the personalities that you worked with, but most of the time they were pleasant. Very seldom did we have any temperamental outbursts, but we did have the freedom of exchanging ideas of how we were going to handle the picture."

Minnelli wanted to film several sequences in Paris, most especially the sequence on the Quai where Kelly and Leslie Caron dance and she begins to fall in love with him. Once again, the front office nixed the idea because it would be too expensive, and Minnelli, Gibbons, and Ames were faced with the task of re-creating Paris on the MGM lot. Ames sketched out a number of scenes, and at a meeting in Gibbons's office, he said, "Okay, on a stage we'll create Notre Dame, a bridge, a quai and Gene Kelly [will] do his dance number with Leslie Caron. Well, everybody thought I was crazy." Freed and Kelly insisted that this one number had to be shot on location in Paris, and Freed was ready to go to the front office to get budgetary permission. Ames stopped them dead by asking Kelly, "Have you ever danced on cobblestones?" Kelly was convinced he could, but everyone else was skeptical and the set was eventually built on Stage 30.

Once the decision was made to shoot the entire film in the studio, Alan A. Antik, the art department's technical advisor, said his job became "monstrous." The technical advisor's job at a studio such as MGM was to ensure that whatever was represented or rendered in a production—unless it was a fantasy—was accurate. Antik, Ames, and Gibbons felt that since this would be a story about the trials and tribulations of a young American artist who decides to stay in Paris after the war and falls in love, the film's sets should look romantic but also as realistic as possible. Minnelli didn't agree. He imagined Paris in the film as looking as stylized as the Caribbean sets in *The Pirate*. Antik remembers having sessions every day with Gibbons, production manager Joe Cohn, Ames, Freed, and Minnelli. "Every day I would see Minnelli," he said, "I would come to his office and he was almost to the point of being rude to me, but I just swallowed it all the time and said, 'That's all right.' Minnelli visualized *An American in Paris* as a glorious musical comedy, that the streets of Paris were full of nothing but pushcarts, with people selling flowers . . . he visualized a sort of Radio City Music Hall production with girls, and all the men wearing a mustache and a beret. The whole thing was too much."

Eventually a compromise was reached, and the big ballet sequence that Minnelli planned for the end of the film was executed as a stylized interpretation of various French artistic movements, with homages to the styles of Renoir, Rousseau, van Gogh, Toulouse-Lautrec, Utrillo, and Dufy. And in Ames, Minnelli found an art director who was as sensitive and as uncompromising as he was regarding the smallest of details. "There were certain things that I wanted to do which involved what I call 'Mickey Mouse' details," said Ames, "but to Vincente and me they were equally important. Just as a sample—grills. There's a kind of grill that the French use which is about 8 or 9 inches high, that cuts off the ground floor window . . . those are the little 'Mickey Mouse' things that I worked like hell to make so that they'd look real. A stairway in the pension, which was worn down, I had so real that poor Oscar Levant refused to go up and down the stairs."

Preparing the black-and-white artists ball for *An American in Paris*.

Even so, this did not head off a clash between the two men that might have ended their professional relationship. Minnelli was troubled about how to stage a masked ball sequence that preceded the fantasy ballet. The ballet was planned to be a riot of color, and Minnelli was afraid its effect would be diluted by the masked ball. When he came up with the idea of doing the ball entirely in black and white it was, he later said, "the greatest moment of my life." But once again there was a communication breakdown. Ames had been a graduate student at the Ecole des Beaux Arts and had attended several artists balls, in which all the participants were masked. He conceived the scene as he remembered it: very colorful and crazy. But when he presented his conception to Minnelli, the director "threw up his arms in horror! That I should even dare consider this kind of a thing! He knew what he wanted later on for the ballet, but at this point he could not tell

One of the forty- by four-hundred-foot paintings used as décor in *An American in Paris*.

us how he wanted to build this ballet to a crescendo of the ultimate in color. So, Minnelli brought in Jack Martin Smith to design the ball." But the relationship was repaired. Minnelli, like Gibbons, knew talent when he saw it. Ames would continue to work with Minnelli on *The Band Wagon*, *Brigadoon*, *The Cobweb* (1955), *Kismet* (1955), *Lust for*

Life (1956), *Designing Woman* (1957), and *Gigi* (1958). It clearly became a professional relationship that was beneficial to both men.

Gibbons had already retired when Ames did some of his best work for Minnelli. Years later, after the MGM backlot had been sold, he grew nostalgic when he recalled what the MGM art department had achieved. Once he received a phone call from someone who, after seeing *An American in Paris* on television, wanted to know what the studio had done with the paintings used in the ballet. "They couldn't appreciate the fact that the paintings were forty by four hundred feet. To them, they were just Utrillos or Toulouse-Lautrecs or something. That's why I say when we started out we really went gung ho—a crazy idea that we never let go of. It was something!"

CHAPTER NINE

A MODERNE LOVE STORY

A modernist masterpiece that was initially given impetus by six cypress trees was, in its final incarnation, inspired by a long, cool woman in a white dress, cut on the bias.

BY 1928 CEDRIC GIBBONS HAD BEEN IN LOS Angeles for almost a decade and head of the art department at Metro-Goldwyn-Mayer for almost three years. After living in a succession of apartment hotels and renting a small bungalow in the hills above Sunset Boulevard, he began to think about building a home of his own. Experiencing a sense of professional security at MGM that he had rarely felt during his years at Goldwyn, in the summer of 1929 he began to scout vacant land for sale in Malibu, Santa Monica, and Pacific Palisades. The lot he eventually purchased in Santa Monica Canyon was small— approximately six acres—but it was bordered in the back by a thick grove of Leyland cypress trees. This particular species of cypress grows in a uniform, symmetrical shape that creates a dense, living wall, perfect for the kind of privacy that Gibbons was seeking.

Cedric Gibbons and Dolores del Río, photographed by Clarence Sinclair Bull shortly after their marriage in 1930.

Many homes built for members of the movie colony in and around Los Angeles during the 1920s and '30s tended to flaunt a merry, meretricious extravagance. Architects such as Wallace Neff and James Dolena became rich designing a succession of Spanish haciendas, French chateaus, and Federal revival and Regency houses for the likes of Constance Bennett, George Cukor, and Claudette Colbert. Gibbons, however, was after something entirely different in the home he planned for himself. He was eager to apply some of the common themes of modern architecture that he had been experimenting with on the sound stages at MGM: the use of industrially produced materials and the adoption of the machine aesthetic; a visual emphasis on vertical and horizontal lines; walls at ninety-degree angles to one another; and finally, the elimination of unnecessary detail and a simplicity and clarity of forms.

As he sketched ideas, however, he soon discovered that the process of planning, designing, and overseeing the construction of a house made demands on his time that he could not easily afford. A fully engaged architect will generally advise on the award of a project to a general contractor, assess the progress of the work during actual construction, and evaluate contractor shop drawings and other submissions. Gibbons's position at MGM did not allow him the time he would need to properly supervise such an undertaking. Enter from screen right, then, a young architect named Douglas Honnold.

A 1924 graduate of Cornell and the architecture school at UC Berkeley, Honnold began work as a draftsman at Witmer and Watson in Los Angeles upon commencement, later becoming a full-fledged architect under the tutelage of such major architectural figures of the period as George Washington Smith and John Parkinson. He was twenty-eight years old in 1929, the year he opened his own firm and met Cedric Gibbons.

The timing was opportune for both men. Honnold scored a commission for a celebrity dwelling that was sure to receive media exposure, a decided coup for his new company, and Gibbons was assured that, as a budding architect yet to establish his own, independent reputation, Honnold would be flexible and not try to modify or otherwise significantly alter Gibbons's vision in order to showcase his own. A synergistic partnership was the last thing he had in mind. As construction got underway, however, Gibbons would meet someone who would unwittingly exert a more powerful influence over his final design than any architect he might engage.

Like millions of other moviegoers, Cedric Gibbons first encountered Dolores del Río on the screen. After being discovered in Mexico by director Edwin Carewe in 1924, Dolores was soon promoted to American audiences as a sort of female Valentino in films such as *What Price Glory?* (1926) and *Resurrection* (1927). In the fall of 1928, she was loaned to MGM to replace an ailing Renée Adorée in Clarence Brown's production of *The Trail of '98*. Almost every day during the film's production, Gibbons would eschew lunch in the executive dining room at the MGM commissary and go to the set to watch del Río work. One afternoon he told Clarence Brown that he wanted to meet her, but the director laughed him off, telling Gibbons that the actress was most assuredly not his type. "She's cold and rather lifeless," he warned. But Gibbons was unconvinced. "Not with those black eyes," he reportedly said. What Brown didn't know at the time was that Dolores was going through a painful divorce from her husband, Jaime del Río, as well as experiencing calculated harassment from Carewe, who was trying to control her career. Both of these developments affected her demeanor on the set, and Gibbons never did manage an introduction.

In the summer of 1930, Gibbons and del Río nearly crossed paths again at a party given by Fredric March. As with so many large Hollywood gatherings (two hundred people had been invited), it was covered by the press. Journalist Julia Lang Hunt described Del Rio's arrival, fashionably late:

> Suddenly a wave of silence enveloped the scene. Glasses were suspended in midair. Sentences were left unfinished. Four hundred eyes were riveted on the doorway, staring at a slender young woman dressed in clinging white satin with the face of a Da Vinci Madonna and the

figure of a marble goddess. For fifteen full seconds the spirited throng was held silent and motionless by the beauty of Dolores del Río.

Two of those four hundred eyes belonged to Cedric Gibbons, and while he could not hope to get Dolores alone that night, he immediately hatched a plan. Soon after the party, he asked two friends of del Río's, the actress Marion Davies and her benefactor William Randolph Hearst, for an introduction. A week later, the two finally met face-to-face at a weekend party held at San Simeon, Hearst's elaborate estate outside San Luis Obispo.

After lunch on Saturday, Gibbons asked Dolores whether or not she liked animals, and when he received an affirmative nod in response, he squired her around Hearst's private zoo, among the largest in the country. The two were seated together at dinner, and by the time they arrived back in Los Angeles by train late Sunday afternoon, they had made a date to have lunch together at MGM the following day.

It was a whirlwind courtship. Six weeks to the day after their introduction, Cedric proposed, on July 31, 1930. Not less than a week later they were married. Father Augustine Hobrecht, a Franciscan Superior at the 150-year-old Santa Barbara mission, performed the ceremony. According to press reports at the time, "only the altar lights, which have burned since Fathers Junipero Serra and Juan Lasuen built the mission in 1784, illuminated the scene."

On the sixth day of her honeymoon, however, Dolores quite suddenly fell ill, possibly from ptomaine poisoning. The infection eventually affected her kidneys, causing dangerously high temperatures. She was bedridden for months. In November 1930, she was admitted to Good Samaritan Hospital in Los Angeles for surgery, and while hospitalized and unable to receive visitors, Gibbons wrote her a letter that still survives in the Del Rio archives in Mexico:

> It seems strange to be writing you; it makes me feel you're far away somewhere and this is the poor substitute for speech. And it is the first time of many times to come I write the words I love you darling at the thought of your love for me.

Gibbons and Del Rio on their wedding day.

I stopped by the house on my way home tonight. I'm making some changes to the original design. I want it to be a wedding gift for you, the perfect setting for the most beautiful woman in the world.

And so a house that was initially given impetus by six cypress trees was, in its final incarnation, inspired by a long cool, woman in a white satin dress, cut on the bias. Initial sketches for the structure reveal that Gibbons was not, on the surface, an architectural innovator. His debt to Richard Neutra and Rudolf Schindler is clear in the use of rectilinear form and smooth surfaces completely stripped of applied ornamentation. The entrance, which faces east, is austere and even severe, an imposing hulk that partially

Unremarkable from the outside, this is the house as it looked shortly after Gibbons and Del Rio moved in. MGM sent studio photographer Clarence Sinclair Bull to take photos for possible publication.

resembled one of the massive sound stages that were rising on the MGM lot around the same time. Except for two small windows that let daylight into Dolores's dressing room on the second floor, the entire front of the house is blank and windowless. When Gibbons and del Río lived there, massive gates of solid, glistening steel barred the entrance and could be opened only by a mechanism within the front door. This was not a house that offered a welcoming invitation to the casual passerby.

The front door seemed like another obstacle one had to maneuver and bore a stark similarity to an entrance a person might expect to find on a bank vault. It was made of Monel, a combination of nickel alloys and copper that are resistant to corrosion, as if the building were planned and constructed to eternally protect something of great value. It is only when one advances toward this door, however, that the visitor can begin to discern exactly what Gibbons is doing. It is placed off-center in a series of shallow setbacks, seven in all, which echo a fluted pattern in the gate. Stepping inside, guests are immediately confronted with an immense eight-foot tall leaded window that offers a glimpse of the greenery in the back of the house, and the approach Gibbons has taken soon becomes clear. As architecture critic Paul Goldberger wrote in his assessment of the

The entrance today. As architecture critic Paul Goldberger has noted, the house is a study in setbacks.

residence in the *New York Times*, "The whole house is an essay in the composition of setbacks, those forms that so preoccupied the 1930s and here have been taken to a considerable level of sophistication. Geometric solids and voids, pulsating with energy, are evident everywhere; it is a kind of celebration of the American moderne style, the showy, flashy style influenced by Art Deco but far sleeker and less decorative."

The layout of the interior augments these ideas. In contrast to the bare, clean void of stucco that sweeps across the front of the house, great steel-framed windows form an expanse along the rear of the first floor and invite the dripping green of pepper trees and the blaze of the western sky into the room. Half partitions and low divisions of polished wood cut the floor space into nooks and alcoves that create little rooms within the larger space, affording spots of privacy.

The main living area was divided into a series of nooks and crannies with sofas and bookshelves.

Gibbons and del Río at home.

But the larger layout brought forth puzzled reactions in the 1930s and even today. Paul Goldberger was vexed in his *Times* appraisal: "The floor plan by itself is intriguing—what exactly was Gibbons trying to say by placing the major entertaining room upstairs beside the master bedroom?" Hollywood journalist Dorothy Calhoun was similarly baffled in 1934. "In this startling house," she wrote, "it is difficult to give some of the rooms conventional names. Certainly, the great apartment into which the visitor first steps is not a hall, reception room, parlor, living room or drawing room."

In fact, it was all of these things and more. Across the back of the room the cold gleam of a metal balustrade anchored a staircase that rose in a series of steps and platforms to the living room—and primary entertaining space—on the second floor. It was a staircase designed for grand entrances, and this first-floor great room was one of the major changes Gibbons made to the blueprint after he wooed and won del Río. As her guests assembled on the first floor, one might imagine Max von Mayerling from *Sunset Boulevard* announcing, "This is the staircase of the palace. Down below, they're waiting for the princess!" It was the focal point of the room, and during a party it offered guests a myriad of opportunities to stage their own pageant as they moved throughout the house. Set off by floor-to-ceiling windows, on choice nights the moon filtered in between the Venetian blinds, offering a natural, diffused backlight.

Looking about this immense space today, restored to its original oyster-white color, it is easy to picture Dolores del Río—dark, exotic down to her crimson fingernails, and with a complexion at once cream and dusky white and ivory—holding court accentuated against the black terrazzo floor and scalloped ceiling. In the evening, she would be lit by all manner of light fixtures recessed on the underside of the grand staircase and glowing softly from coves and recesses.

Off the main room on the first floor could be found a medium-sized library, dining and breakfast rooms, a kitchen, a bedroom,

The staircase as photographed by Bull in the 1930s.

and Gibbons's office/workshop. The grand staircase led visitors across the back of the library and up to a huge, twenty-five- by forty-five-foot living room. Most visitors were invariably surprised to discover, above and beyond the divans on the second floor, endless bookcases rising to the ceiling. There is a terrace off the living room and also a separate wing that was given over to Dolores del Río's bedroom suite. It consisted of a dressing room in dull silver and black, with glass shelves that held an array of perfume bottles. A row of silver lamps on the ceiling cast the light upward. A single chair of silver with white cushions was the only movable object in the bedroom when del Río occupied it. A white satin-covered bed built into the paneling, and a long, glass dressing table, resting as crystal columns would, were the only other pieces of furniture in the room.

The dining room as it looked in the 1990s, with the staircase to the living room in the background.

The long expanse of the living area with a peek into Cedric's office/den.

When the house was built, Gibbons made sure that nothing would detract or distract from his design. The most utilitarian objects went unrecognized. Parallel planes of narrow steel turned out to be a radiator. Swinging screens of metal mesh covered fireplaces. And no faucets marred the luster of the black marble bathroom, walled with mirrors, in which del Río bathed. Silver disks in the floor, activated like pedals, sent water into the tub or sink. Further, if there was any lingering doubt that this was indeed the boudoir of a movie queen, the heads of the screws holding the mirrors to the wall were shaped like stars. In the summer, a mechanical device dripped chilled water onto the roof, creating an artificial rain shower to cool the interior.

As in Richard Neutra's Lovell House, built in 1927, the straight line dominates the entire structure, and the heady, sensuous curvature found in many streamlined structures erected in the 1930s and '40s is conspicuously missing. Doorways are accented by cascades of retreating rectangles or by inverted staircases, hung upside down, with the face of each step illuminated by electric lighting concealed behind translucent glass panels. But while the gleam of chrome, iridescent glass, and polished Bakelite dominate, the house was by no means devoid of color when Gibbons and del Río lived there. It was everywhere, and ascendant in the more recessed light of evening. At the right of the front door, as one entered, the partition was a mottled plum color. Beyond, against the wall, was a large painting in a silver frame with three surfaces, its focal point a jar of lush violet orchids.

Upstairs, the couches that lined the walls and surrounded the alcoves were a dull red color, while downstairs a gunmetal blue shade was employed. If these colors became subtle and evanescent during the day, when sunlight flooded the great rooms, it was because everything was washed in shades of green from the garden—from the olive green of the eucalyptus to the brilliant green of the palms and the dark green of the cypress that first attracted Gibbons to the property. The vegetation was so overpowering that one columnist, viewing a photo of Cedric and Dolores in front of a back window with a tree branch hovering above them, suggested that the couple might be living in a treehouse for all anyone knew.

The gardens encircled a pool and tennis court, as well as a changing room, that were a crucial part of the grounds. Gibbons belonged to a motion picture tennis club that held a tournament every year in which cameramen, assistant directors, and property boys faced off against stars, executives, and directors. The pre-tourney preparations took place on the Gibbons's sunken court, one of the best private courts in Southern California, and

The back of the house as it looks today, with a view of the swimming pool where Garbo once swam.

Sunday afternoon brunches often found Ronald Colman, Richard Barthelmess, Robert Montgomery, John Gilbert, Fredric March, Edmund Lowe, Warner Baxter, and Ben Lyon practicing their backhands. Very occasionally, Greta Garbo would drop by unannounced during the week and shyly ask if she and a companion might play tennis. She appreciated the privacy afforded by cypress trees and high walls too.

For more formal occasions the dining room featured an oblong table of pebbled glass two inches thick that seated twelve. Walls of the prevalent putty tone that graced the majority of the rooms were offset by ceiling-high windows overlooking the terraces and gardens and draped in folds of gold duvetyn. Paneled mirrors and steps of glass lights down one side of the ceiling reflected the table's appointments.

A view of the tennis court from the second floor.

During their marriage Gibbons and his wife employed a staff of six, including a cook, housekeeper, and full-time gardener—a sizable number considering the house was by no means enormous. Its look of ample, sweeping space is achieved through cunning illusion, fostered by the use of expanses of bare wall, half-partitions, mirrors, and above all, massive windows. As Dorothy Calhoun wrote, "it was planned and built to be lived in by two people and only two."

This fact later played into the hands of Hollywood revisionists who used it as "evidence" that this was a marriage of convenience, and that Gibbons and del Río both may have been gay. The fact that they had separate bedrooms only added fuel to the fire.

But the quirky melodrama of the couple's sleeping arrangements, to use author Adrian Tinniswood's phrase, "reached a peak" in yet another novelty Cedric added to the house after he married Dolores: Access from Gibbons's bedroom on the ground floor to del Río's on the floor above was achieved by means of a clandestine passage that led to a trapdoor. A similar contrivance was used in the construction of the Maison de Verre, a collaboration between Dutch architect Bernard Bijvoet and interior designer Pierre Chareau that was built in Paris between 1928 and 1932. It is entirely possible that Gibbons knew about the Paris house, which was attracting a great deal of attention in the architectural press at the time. Or perhaps his first and only inspiration was again Dolores del Río, who explained to a reporter from *Modern Screen* in 1935, "We live like lovers—deliberately!"

There is an instantly recognizable flair for the dramatic about the house Gibbons created, and it was the perfect setting for a theatrical movie queen who knew the value of a perfectly timed entrance. It was self-conscious and yet severely simple and pragmatic; no overwhelming detail obtrudes on the flow of ideas inherent in the design. It held the world at bay with imposing walls, steel gates, and heavy, obdurate doors, but once you were granted access, it was the most convivial place imaginable, with books at every hand as well as cozy alcoves complete with divans and fireplaces. Sunshine flooded every nook and cranny of the main rooms. Gibbons undoubtedly learned from the International Style houses of the 1920s that preceded his, but he added a lilt and a kick to its rectilinear aesthetic and created, as Paul Goldberger has written, "a certain type of Hollywood glamour at no cost to its basic intentions."

Gibbons with his first Oscar, awarded for his work on *The Bridge of San Luis Rey* in 1929. One of the founding members of the Academy of Motion Picture Arts and Sciences, Gibbons is credited with designing the Academy Award.

EPILOGUE

WHEN THE LEGEND BECOMES FACT, print the legend." By definition, a legend is a nonhistorical or unverifiable story that is popularly accepted as fact. And perhaps the most famous and persistent professional legend associated with Gibbons, one that has been handed down and repeated endlessly for decades, is the notion that he was inspired to create the art deco sets for *Our Dancing Daughters* after visiting the Exposition Internationale des Arts Décoratifs et Industriels Modernes, held in Paris in 1925. The exposition ran from April through October and was conceived by the French government to highlight the new art deco style in architecture, interior design, furniture, glass, jewelry, and other decorative arts. The odds that Gibbons would have been able to find the time in his professional schedule in 1925 to attend this exposition are, however, slim to none.

In 1925 Gibbons was not working in a supervisory capacity in the MGM art department and was, indeed, fending off a potential rival in Romain de Tirtoff. In addition, Gibbons designed, alone or in tandem with another designer such as Joseph Wright, Merrill Pye, or Richard Day, a total of twenty films that year: *His Secretary*; *Lights of Old Broadway*; *The Masked Bride*; *Exchange of Wives*; *Daddy's Gone A-Hunting*; *The Mystic*; *Pretty Ladies*; *Fine Clothes*; *The Sporting Venus*; *A Slave of Fashion*; *The Way of a Girl*; *The Denial*; *The Great Divide*; *Cheaper to Marry*; *Excuse Me*; *Bright Lights*; *Man and Maid*; *Sally, Irene, and Mary*; *The Merry Widow*; and *Confessions of a Queen*. This averages out to almost two films per month for the entire year, not taking into account the work Thalberg summoned Gibbons to do when *Ben-Hur* was brought back to Culver City. A trip to Paris leaving from Los Angeles in the mid-1920s would necessitate a cross-country train trip to New York followed by a transatlantic crossing and back again. That Gibbons would have had time available to allot to such a trip considering his work schedule seems, in retrospect, virtually impossible. And realistically, it would have been unnecessary as well. The rudiments of art deco design were hardly unknown in America in the late 1920s; in New York City, especially, many of the leading department stores had staged exhibits and model rooms by leading European practitioners of the movement, one or two years before *Our Dancing Daughters* went into production.

As Marilyn Friedman notes in her book *Making America Modern*, in 1927 and 1928 there were exhibitions of modern design in department stores all over the country, sparked by those at Lord and Taylor and R. H. Macy & Co., in Manhattan, and Abraham & Straus and Frederick Loeser & Co., in Brooklyn. In 1927, Marshall Field and Company in Chicago organized several exhibitions of modern design, which were followed in department stores located in Boston, Milwaukee, Atlanta, and Pittsburgh. In addition, a collection of four hundred objects from the 1925 Paris exhibition toured museums across the United States beginning in 1926. To be exposed to the fundamentals of the art deco movement,

Gibbons need not have visited the exhibition in Paris. But the story endures, as do many others.

For example, according to John Hambley and Patrick Downing in *The Art of Hollywood*, "stories abound of Gibbons stopping important productions because no BWS (big white set) had been designed for them." This seems highly implausible when every set design was approved by Gibbons before a film even went into production. In another vein, it was said that the unit art directors who worked under Gibbons called him "Gibby" behind his back, but "would never have dared to address him this way to his face." This reinforces the image of the austere and remote executive, secretly ridiculed behind his back, but ignores the fact that Gibbons himself signed most of his interoffice correspondence with the appellation "Gibby." Nor does it acknowledge the last birthday card he received from former members of his staff on March 20, 1959: "Dear Gibby," it read, "it gives us pleasure and happiness to wish you a very happy birthday, which again brings to our minds the many enjoyable years spent as your associates." It was signed by Hans Peters, Arnold "Buddy" Gillespie, George Gibson, Preston Ames, Edward Carfagno, and Merrill Pye.

As late as 1951, only four years short of Gibbons's retirement from MGM, a story in the *Cleveland Plain Dealer* continued to mythologize Gibbons's past, identifying Gibbons's father with the first name "Adrian" and maintaining that the late Thomas A. Edison was so impressed with a copy of an El Greco canvas Gibbons had painted that he gave him a position in the Bedford Park Edison Studios in 1911, adding still more unverified information and easily disproven fictions to his professional and personal dossier. Even after his retirement, *Hollywood Studio Magazine*, in an article titled "Cedric Gibbons MGM Art Director, 1924–1956," recorded that "the considerable wealth of his family allowed Cedric to be educated privately by tutors. Realizing his interest in architecture his family sent Gibbons to the old continent to study the history of architecture and its national characteristics. He visited England, France, Italy, and Spain."

Many people have also weighed in with their own opinions and judgments about Cedric Gibbons's working methods and accomplishments, and the "traditional story" weaves a tale that too often diminishes his achievements.

"At MGM it was make everybody feel good," art director Robert Boyle, who started his career at Paramount during World War II, told an interviewer in the 1970s. "Gibbons and those people didn't care about realism. At MGM shopgirls lived in penthouses. . . . Cedric Gibbons had people who did his bidding. They couldn't vary from his stamp; they knew where they were." Boyle never worked at MGM, but those who did—and stayed for decades—vehemently refute this last statement, an easy and facile dismissal of the actual working conditions in the MGM art department, and the designs it produced. Years after his retirement, Randall Duell stated that "at Metro, at that time, they were doing about fifty-some-odd pictures a year, and we had about fifteen art directors, so there was a need for a head. Gibbons was a fine person to work for and work with, and I enjoyed every minute I worked with him. He was a talented man—high imagination—and he always stimulated you to think a little deeper. We had complete freedom. After all, he was looking for ideas too." And the shopgirls played by Joan Crawford, Dorothy Sebastian, and Anita Page in *Our Blushing Brides* or Constance Bennett in *The Easiest Way* would most likely have preferred living in a penthouse instead of the crowded tenement flats Gibbons and his associates created for their characters to inhabit, at least before they met the rich men who were in a position to elevate their standard of living. (In *Faithless*, released in 1931, Tallulah Bankhead traveled a different path, going from wealthy heiress to a down-and-out prostitute living in a cheap apartment hotel.) It would most certainly not describe the small one-room apartment Gibbons designed for John and Mary Sims (James Murray and Eleanor Boardman) in King Vidor's *The Crowd* (1928), with its Murphy bed and exposed toilet. After its release, Louis B. Mayer would continually refer to *The Crowd* as "that goddamned toilet picture."

John and Mary Sims (Eleanor Boardman and James Murray) in their tiny apartment next to an elevated train. *The Crowd* received a number of nominations at the very first Academy Awards presentation in 1928. In 1989, the film was one of the first twenty-five motion pictures to be selected for preservation in the United States National Film Registry by the Library of Congress. Gibbons's realistic designs, along with Arnold Gillespie's special effects in the Coney Island sequence, have certainly played a part in the film's enduring reputation.

Director Mitchell Leisen did work at MGM, and left with a very dim view of its supervising art director:

> The distinct Metro style was set up by Cedric Gibbons. . . . Whether it fit the story or not, he was going to have his sets paramount. In *Young Man*, we were supposed to have a dinner party at a gold club in Billings, Montana. I picked out a set that was standing and we had the people all ready to go in business suits but, oh no, that was not

When John returns home drunk one evening, photography director Henry Sharp created expressionistic shadows that contributed to the gloom and desolation of the set.

MGM. Gibbons did the most elaborate country club you've ever seen, all bright white and everybody dressed to the teeth in white tie and tails. Then one scene took place in a bookie joint. We used some tacky real estate office on Washington Boulevard for the exterior, but when Gibbons did the interior, it looked like something out of *House and Garden*. He had copper lamps with plants growing out of them. In a bookie joint! He was God out there. He wanted it a certain way, that was the MGM style, and that's what you got.

A cursory viewing of the film Leisen refers to, *Young Man with Ideas* (1952), starring Glenn Ford and Ruth Roman, reveals a country club set that looks pleasant but hardly lavish. No one in the scene wears formal attire, and it lasts no longer than five or ten minutes at the outside. And the bookie joint Leisen describes does not appear in the film, although there is always the possibility the scene was filmed and later excised in the cutting room.

In 1941 Edwin Willis waxed enthusiastic over the letters he had received—they filled an entire filing cabinet—from all over the country asking about the furnishings in the remake of *When Ladies Meet* and where they could be purchased. "Decorators have told me," Willis said, "that after the release of *When Ladies Meet*, requests for Early Americana tripled." At the same time, he noted that "when there is an opportunity, the sets are keyed to budget incomes. The film *Keeping Company* (1940) is a pleasant little story about a pair of newlyweds [played by Ann Rutherford and John Shelton]. When the

The pleasant but hardly lavish country club set in *Young Man with Ideas*.

In what may be called a "small white set," the kitchen where Ann Rutherford and John Shelton begin their married life in *Keeping Company* is decidedly simple.

apartment which they shared was decorated, only those items which could be purchased comfortably from a $100 a week income were used."

If a character was rich, it showed on the screen, but aside from most musicals with their whimsical plots, imaginary locales, and extravagant production numbers, realism was the MGM style and, with few exceptions, that's what you got. There is little doubt that Gibbons, as well as Gilbert Adrian, could behave like a martinet at times. As George Cukor said when discussing the department heads at MGM, "Like a lot of people who have been in the forefront of a movement, if they stick to it, they become rather old-fashioned." But when Cukor wanted Paul Huldschinsky to work as an art director on *Gaslight*, he got him; Minnelli and Gibbons came to respect each other's talents and forged a friendship and working relationship that lasted over fifteen years.

In 1957 the celebrated French film critic André Bazin wrote, "The American cinema is a classical art, but why not admire in it what is most admirable, i.e., not only the talent of this or that filmmaker, but the genius of the system . . . ?" Irving Thalberg, more so than any other Hollywood "mogul," generally receives the most credit for putting this system in place and streamlining it until it became a self-sufficient mode of production for almost three decades. Cedric Gibbons installed a facsimile of it in the largest single autonomous department at MGM, and he survived Thalberg by twenty years and Louis B. Mayer by five years. He hired some of the best talent that was available at the time, then nurtured it and stimulated his people to create their best work. Those who claim Gibbons just supervised and never created anything forget his formative years at Goldwyn, or the films he took on as more or less personal projects, such as *Grand Hotel* or *Marie Antoinette*. And as supervisory art director, most accounts of his career do not consider the substantial amount of work he had to do to keep the system running, dealing with budgets and the allocation of production space. For while MGM was a studio known for its largesse, financial considerations still had to be taken into account.

Marie Antoinette is a good example. The estimate that Gibbons made for the cost of constructing the Dauphin's apartment, for instance, was $2,680, but production manager Joe W. Finn estimated the final cost to be $2,888. As a result, Gibbons made every effort to cut costs for Marie's apartment, study, bedroom, and anteroom. Its designated cost was $15,000 but it came in for $14,264, which gave Gibbons leeway to allocate money toward other expenses on the film. In 1944, when the construction of St. Louis Street for *Meet Me in St. Louis* topped two hundred thousand dollars and almost gave Mayer a heart attack, Gibbons was able to save a large amount of money by redressing the "Wimpole Street" set for *Gaslight* the following year, reducing the estimate for the set from $102,148 to $21,801. He was also, on occasion, able to poke fun at the entire process. "All of the art department," he wrote to MGM producers Ulrich Busch and Charles Chic in 1938, "every soul in the art department, is waiting for that day when some member of the production department thinks we have not allowed enough money. Because in preliminary set estimates we are so often on the high side, I cannot but believe that occasionally we are below. And as I look back at the dim vistas of years past, I know with regret, that we have sometimes been under. Go with God! Gibby."

Cedric Gibbons resigned his position at MGM due to ill health on April 26, 1956. The resignation notice was brief and addressed to Loew's Incorporated in Culver City:

> Gentlemen: This is to inform you that I have decided to terminate my employment with Loew's Incorporated at this time. In accordance with this decision, I am applying to the Loew's Retirement Plan Committee for the benefits to which I am entitled under the Loew's Retirement Plan.

William Horning replaced Gibbons as head of an art department that would not last much longer than another decade. The move was prescient in some ways. Gibbons would win his eleventh and final Academy Award the following year, along with unit art director Malcolm Brown (who began as a sketch artist on *The Wizard of Oz*) for Robert Wise's *Somebody Up There Likes Me*. The film starred Paul Newman and Pier Angeli in the story of boxer Rocky Graziano. But, as was becoming increasing common, Robert Wise took his company to New York City for several weeks of location shooting while MGM's "New York Street" stood idle on the backlot. "To get authentic settings," said Wise, "we filmed in and around Brooklyn and the Lower East Side, the actual locales where Graziano lived

Pier Angeli and Paul Newman filming on the streets of New York City.

during the 1920s and 1940s." The director found, however, that in many of the tenement sections whole blocks had been torn down, replaced by modern housing projects. Television aerials also presented a problem, as did getting City Hall and the New York Police Department to cooperate with the company and clear blocks for filming. But these were growing pains, before city and state film commissions were formed to encourage and facilitate location filming.

In their book *Sets in Motion: Art Direction and Film Narrative*, Charles and Mirella Jona Affron wrote that "in the United States, 1960 closes the decade-long decline of the studio system that had ruled production since the early 1920s." It is somehow both ironic and poignant, then, that Cedric Gibbons passed that same year, on July 26, after a long illness. Ten years hence, on May 4, 1970, the first day of a three-day auction would put forty years' worth of MGM props and décor up for bid. "How much do we hear?" the auctioneer David Weisz asked as he faced a crowd of nearly five thousand people that first morning on Sound Stage 30, where the Yellow Brick Road once wound its way under the klieg lights. A picture of a cut crystal decanter flashed on the screen behind him. Starting with a bid of ten dollars, it eventually sold for ninety dollars, the first of more than twenty-five thousand items emptied from the storehouse started by Edwin Willis and Gibbons more than forty years earlier. Before the decade was out, the fabled backlot, including St. Louis Street, the Andy Hardy house, Brownstone Street, Fifth Avenue, Small Town Square, and Wimpole Street would all be bulldozed into dust to make way for a housing development.

"The beauty of Cedric Gibbons," said Preston Ames a few years before the backlot was demolished, "was that he allocated responsibility and then allowed you to proceed with that responsibility. If you wanted help you went for help. If you were in trouble, you explained your case and he judged you accordingly. If you were right, he would back you up to the hilt; if you were wrong, he would forgive you. Secondly, he didn't want you to be just a pretty picture maker. That he loathed. He felt that was being a little unfair to yourself and that it was being unfair to the director. If you couldn't take that sketch and make it into reality, you were just an artist. And that he wouldn't tolerate."

Elmer Grey, a noted Southern California architect responsible for, among other buildings, the Beverly Hills Hotel, had this to say after visiting the MGM lot in 1935:

> There are no schools turning out art directors by the hundreds. They are self-made, and producers do well to accord them recognition on the screen. To their skill much of the success of modern picture making is due. They have it in their hands to increase enormously an appreciation and enjoyment of good architecture among the masses. The buildings they depict are not permanent to be sure, but they reach many more people with their message than do many permanent

buildings, and often in ways that make very lasting impressions. It must be gratifying to feel that one is composing pictures which, in their ultimate life-like realism, enthrall and instruct audiences of thousands the world over.

On June 12, 1950, Gibbons received a letter from Norman Lowenstein, president of the Art Directors Guild. "On the evening of June 8, 1950," it read, "at the society's regular quarterly membership meeting in the Bel-Air Hotel, a new society award was established—the Society of Motion Picture Art Directors Medal for Distinguished Achievement. This medal will be presented to art directors who in the society's opinion have done the most to further the art of the motion picture through the medium of art direction. It is my very pleasant duty to inform you that the membership of the Guild unanimously voted to present the first Distinguished Achievement Medal to you."

The award, for "distinguished and meritorious achievement," was presented to Gibbons at a banquet held on October 12, 1950, at the Beverly Wilshire Hotel in Beverly Hills. During the course of the evening, the following telegrams of congratulations Gibbons had received from those who were unable to attend the ceremony were read aloud to those present:

Jack Warner: "Am very happy to learn of the honor that is being accorded to you by the society of motion picture art directors. You are certainly deserving of this recognition and it could not have happened to a nicer guy."

William Cameron Menzies: "Congratulations to my old school mate for joining the immortals of the Art Students League."

Gary Cooper: "His has been a major contribution to the advancement of motion pictures and I am happy that his achievements are being honored by your society."

Louis B. Mayer: "Deeply regret I cannot be with you on this occasion. I share with you great pride in this high honor paid you by your fellow art directors and would like to add my fellow congratulations and sincerest personal felicitations."

Dore Schary: "All of us here at Metro-Goldwyn-Mayer are proud of the achievements of Cedric Gibbons. And we are proud of the recognition being given him tonight by the Art Directors Guild. Gibby is one of the few men of whom it can be said in all honesty that he is a gentleman and a scholar. We know, respect, and love him well here because of his work, because of his impeccable manners and because of his inspirational talent which has made enormous contributions to the Metro-Goldwyn-Mayer program for many, many years."

Cecil B. DeMille: "I second everything Jesse Lasky will say to you for he and I know from our years of working together how much our industry owes to the creative talents of art directors and how thoroughly deserved is the honor you are paying Cedric Gibbons, one of the most distinguished members of your profession in Hollywood."

Jack Martin Smith: "Greetings from Dixie. All of us from south of the Mason-Dixon line send congratulations to you on your great record of achievement."

Edward Carfagno: "Best wishes for a fine and well-deserved evening."

Vincente Minnelli: "Dear Gibby: And I think so too!"

Upon accepting his award, the speech Gibbons gave was short, focusing on the future rather than the past:

> I have been told that when the art directors decided to honor one of their own people, my selection was spontaneous and unanimous. For that, you can understand, I am both humble and grateful. This is indeed a great and rare honor.
>
> I believe only art directors in this industry understand the magnitude of the problems we are called upon each day to face and solve. To have this award come from them means more to me than anything that has ever happened in my life. It makes me very proud.
>
> The Society of Motion Picture Art Directors, since its inception has set one of its goals to increase the importance and the understanding of the Art Director's contribution and place in the making

of motion pictures. This, as we know, has been altogether too rare. The Society, I am happy to say, is now well on its way to successfully achieve that result.

But we, as individuals, must further the Society's aim and by our own technical knowledge go beyond the actual set requirements of the script in our preparation and engineering of how the picture will be made, assuming to ourselves in the most co-operative manner, the problems of our director and producer.

Certainly, we know our jobs now go far beyond the designing of sets and I have found in many quarters an increasing comprehension of our very real contribution to the finished picture. Our problem now is not so much educating the public as to our place in the industry but to continue that education within the industry itself.

I thank you.

The "grand old man" of Hollywood art direction,
photographed at home with nine of his eleven Oscars

ACKNOWLEDGMENTS

First and foremost, I want to thank Ms. Faye Thompson at the Margaret Herrick Library of the Academy of Motion Picture Arts and Sciences. Her indefatigable photo research on my behalf helped immeasurably in making this book possible. I also extend my gratitude to John Damer, Elizabeth Cathcart, Jeanie Braun, Taylor Morales, Kristine Krueger, and the librarians at the Academy library, who assisted me as I sifted through countless photographs in their extensive MGM set reference and production collections. Melissa LeBoeuf made procuring photos of the Gibbons house as it looks today an easy and painless process.

Jeffery McGraw (aka "Sprite" Gravier), my former agent, worked tirelessly to find a publisher for this project when the timing wasn't right yet. But he believed in it from the beginning, and I will not forget his efforts on my behalf. I owe a debt of gratitude to Hugh Fordin and Jerome Delamater, who were able to interview many of the unit art directors who worked under Cedric Gibbons and have since passed. Cathy Whitlock made many helpful suggestions as I began to shape the manuscript, and my dear friend Karen Severns read several initial chapters and, as usual, made many insightful comments and suggestions.

And a big thank-you to my editor Rick Rinehart, who felt that the time *was* right.

NOTES

PREFACE

x. *A portentous star rising on the decorating horizon* . . . Stuart, "Movie Set-Up," p. 20.

x. *There is probably no other designer in Hollywood* . . . Eustis, "Designing for the Movies: Gibbons of MGM," p. 783.

x. I must refer to him as the dean of the Hollywood art directors . . . Flint, "Cedric Gibbons," p. 117.

xii. *The art department was what it was* . . . Hall, *Dolores Del Rio: Beauty in Light and Shade*, p. 135.

xiii. *Grass was ripped up* . . . Eyman, *Lion of Hollywood*, p. 143.

xvii. *If imagination is permitted to soar in contemporary settings* . . . Watts, ed., *Behind the Screen: How Films Are Made*, p. 53.

xviii. *Why, in some houses you can actually tell* . . . *Harper's Bazaar*, April 1928, p. 111.

few [houses] are inhabited by individuals . . . *Harper's Bazaar*, May 1929, p. 95.

A set can of itself tell a whole story . . . Metro-Goldwyn-Mayer Exhibitor Pressbook, *Our Modern Maidens*, p. 4.

The man who makes everyone's dreams come true . . . Watts, p. 49.

xix. *You're on your own [today]* . . . Long, Robert, Emmet, ed. *George Cukor: Interviews*, p. 111.

CHAPTER ONE: THE BUILDER'S SON

1. *Telling too many lies* . . . Bret, *Errol Flynn: Gentleman Hellraiser*, p. 100.

Pat Dane asking Slapsy Maxie's band . . . *Los Angeles Times*, June 21, 1941, Part II, p. 9.

3. *Fun's fun, but for the love of God* . . . MGM Art Department Records, Folder 44, "Cedric Gibbons," Academy of Motion Picture Arts and Sciences.

4. *He studied painting in his youth* . . . Crisler, "Dolores and Husband," *New York Times*, February 6, 1938, p. 5.

A star that had first seen the light in Dublin . . . Stuart, "Movie Set-Up," p. 56.

5. *Cedric Gibbons was born at 76 Rush Street in Brooklyn, New York* . . . Letter from Robert Errol to Gibbons, in *Academy of Motion Picture Arts and Sciences Center for Motion Picture Study, Special Collections*, Collection 512, Cedric Gibbons and Hazel Brooks Papers, 1918–1992.

6. *The Irish fill our prisons, our poor houses* . . . *Chicago Evening Post*, 1868, in *Ethnic Chicago: A Multicultural Portrait*, p. 57.

On their marriage certificate, Austin listed his occupation as "builder" . . . Marriage Certificate, Austin P. Gibbons and Veronica F. Fitzpatrick, 3 June 1889, Brooklyn, New York, certificate number 2197, New York Municipal Archives.

7. *Brooklyn had evolved into one of the leading producers of manufactured goods in the nation* . . . *Harper's Monthly*, April 1893, p. 664.

9. *The entire Gibbons household was thrown into a turmoil* . . . Death Certificate, Veronica Florence Fitzpatrick Gibbons, 15 April 1910, State of New York, Certificate Number 1140, New York Municipal Archives.

10. *"If you have any recent photos of yourself*. . . Letter from Robert Errol to Cedric Gibbons dated January 17, 1929, in *Academy of Motion Picture Arts and Sciences Center for Motion Picture Study, Special Collections*, Collection 512, Cedric Gibbons and Hazel Brooks Papers, 1918–1992.

11. *Wouldn't it be ironic if* . . . Ibid.

I am so glad that you saw your father in Chicago . . . Letter from Helen Stewart to Cedric Gibbons dated July 22, 1938, in *Academy of Motion Picture Arts and Sciences Center for Motion Picture Study, Special Collections*, Collection 512, Cedric Gibbons and Hazel Brooks Papers, 1918–1992.

The League had been founded in 1875 by a group of artists . . . Landgren, *Years of Art: The Story of the Art Students League of New York*, Robert M. McBride and Company, 1940.

13. *He recalled years later that Gibbons* . . . *New York Times*, December 17, 1943, p. 27.
    The voice of time remained aloof and unperturbed . . . Jackson ed., *Empire City: New York Through the Centuries*, p. 564.

14. *I duplicated the studio of Jules Adler in Paris* . . . *Sight and Sound*, Winter, 1979/1980, pp. 49–50.

15. *Ballin was weighted down* . . . *Western States Jewish History*, October 1991, p. 3.
    Without its setting, a picture production is hopelessly lost . . . *Los Angeles Times*, April 27, 1919, p. III, 1.
    All traits of character can be convincingly suggested . . . Ibid., p. III, 1.

16. *Altogether this room will be one of the most striking things in America* . . . *Art and Progress*, September 1912, p. 702.
    This was where he had begun his "nefarious career" . . . Letter from Cedric Gibbons to Benjamin P. Schoenfein, Vice President of the Public National Bank and Trust Company of NY dated June 2, 1950, in Academy of Motion Picture Arts and Sciences Center for Motion Picture Study, Special Collections, Collection 512, Cedric Gibbons and Hazel Brooks Papers, 1918–1992.

17. *[striding] down a gangplank in New York* . . . Tungate, *Adland: A Global History of Advertising*, p. 25.
    What Resor called one of his favorite "scientific" devices . . . Fox, *The Mirror Makers*, p. 75.

18. *Resor had "more than a touch of the aristocrat"* . . . Ibid., p. 91.

CHAPTER TWO: WANTED: INTERIOR DESIGNERS FOR THE SCREEN

23. *It is our intention to give the best* . . . *Moving Picture World*, March 9, 1907, p. 4.

24. *The subject is exceptionally well-rendered* . . . *Moving Picture World*, June 27, 1908, p. 548.
    The eventual function of the art director . . . Everson, *American Silent Film*, p. 299.

25. *Good taste is not confined to the homes* . . . Reeves, *Moving Picture World*, June 11, 1911, p. 1760.
    A drawing room covered with "arabesque ornament" . . . Physioc, *Moving Picture World*, May 25, 1912, p. 714.

29. *Here were faces, groups, and interiors lit by a warm glow of light* . . . MacGowan, *Photoplay*, January 1921, p. 74.
    It is with considerable surprise . . . *House Beautiful*, February 1915, p. 82.

31. *In 1910, when I was with Gaumont in Paris* . . . Downing and Hambley, *The Art of Hollywood*, p. 25.
    Some of them came right out of my imagination . . . Ibid., p. 27.

33. *For Hearst, the conclusion was clear* . . . Ramirez, p. 27.
    You are bound to be impressed . . . *New York Times*, September 15, 1922, p. 17.

34. *I want to make pictures* . . . Joseph Urban Papers, Rare Book and Manuscript Archive, Columbia University Libraries.

35. *I was seeking an opportunity* . . . Eyman, *Empire of Dreams: The Epic Films of Cecil B. DeMille*, p. 139.
    Talk to the greatest and most accredited artists . . . Lindsay, *Moving Picture World*, July 21, 1917, p. 368.
    Motion pictures are, or should be, pictorial art . . . Buckland, *Moving Picture World*, July 21, 1917, p. 375.

Every actor is a human pigment . . . Tourneur, *Moving Picture World*, July 21, 1917, p. 378.

36. *Within the past year* . . . *The American Architect*, July 7, 1920, p. 2.

It was something even the legitimate theater . . . MacGowan, *Motion Picture Classic*, March 1919, p. 17.

That halfway ground between reality and romance . . . *The American Architect*, July 7, 1920, p. 5.

CHAPTER THREE: GIBBONS AT GOLDWYN

39. *I have from the very beginning* . . . "No Limits to Field of Pictures," *Motion Picture News*, July 12, 1919, p. 541.

40. *This process* . . . Moses, *Moving Picture World*, July 1917, p. 384.

And it is not without . . . Ibid., p. 386.

A revelation of the high art of the screen . . . *Philadelphia Public Ledger*, October 17, 1917, n.p.

The picture has many distinctions . . . "Both Sides of the Curtain," *Evening Ledger*—Philadelphia, October 20, 1917, p. 18.

42. *The glint of sun* . . . "Goldwyn Buys Triangle Studio," *Motion Picture News*, June 7, 1919, p. 3811.

44. *One year in production* . . . "Goldwyn advertising insert," *Moving Picture World*, July 1920, page 289.

45. *And in which were so illustrated* . . . *New York Times*, August 11, 1920, p. 8.

47. *When the set stands out to such a degree* . . . Lipke, *Los Angeles Times*, April 22, 1923, p. III13.

Six thousand people stormed the box office . . . *New York Morning Telegraph*, September 20, 1920, n.p.

Here, in the motion picture at its best . . . Lachenbruch, *The American Architect*, November 3, 1920, p. 563.

49. *It is well known* . . . *Los Angeles Times*, February 19, 1922, p. VIII5.

50. *First, after reading the story* . . . Ibid.

51. *The soap bubble ballet* . . . *Cumberland Evening Times*, March 2, 1923, page 10.

The settings, designed by Cedric Gibbons . . . *Bradford Era*, December 12, 1921, page 5.

52. *It is my belief* . . . "Use Color in Sets to Aid Actors," *Canton News*, November 18, 1923, n.p.

56. *The war for motion picture supremacy* . . . Berg, *Goldwyn*, p. 88.

CHAPTER FOUR: THE EMERGENCE OF METRO-GOLDWYN-MAYER

59. *Specialization in every phase of production* . . . *Motion Picture News*, February 7, 1925, p. 607.

61. *"Ah! This is the Place!"* . . . *Los Angeles Herald Examiner*, June 7, 1925, n.p.

If the nabob departed . . . *Los Angeles Times*, May 22, 1932, p. 30.

"I came here seven months ago . . ." *Culver City Daily News*, June 20, 1925.

64. *We have some very beautiful sets going up* . . . Bess Meredith letter to Louis B. Mayer, July 14, 1924, Academy of Motion Picture Arts and Sciences Center for Motion Picture Study, Rudy Behlmer Papers, *Ben-Hur*.

The scope and size of the spectacle was there . . . Thomas, *Thalberg: Life and Legend*, p. 55.

I want to say to you that . . . A. S. Aronson letter to Louis B. Mayer, November 1924, Academy of Motion Picture Arts and Sciences Center for Motion Picture Study, Rudy Behlmer Papers, *Ben-Hur*.

I could have made the whole thing . . . Crowther, *The Lion's Share*, p. 97.

At Thalberg's request . . . Academy of Motion Picture Arts and Sciences Center for Motion Picture Study, Rudy Behlmer Papers, *Ben-Hur*.

67. *The audience is going to think* . . . Thomas, p. 57.
69. *The sequence fades in on a line of mounted trumpeters* . . . Brownlow, *The Parade's Gone By*, p. 413.
   We had two little hanging miniatures . . . Ibid., p. 413.
   When the camera photographed the miniature . . . Ibid., p. 413.
74. *The stipulation that it must appear* . . . Academy of Motion Picture Arts and Sciences Center for Motion Picture Study, Special Collections, Cedric Gibbons Contracts Folder.
   Gibbons usually had or shared the credit . . . Deschner, *The Velvet Light Trap*, p. 31.
75. *In a memo dated November 11, 1936* . . . Academy of Motion Picture Arts and Sciences Center for Motion Picture Study, Special Collections, Art Department Records, Folder 65, Set Construction Costs.
   The most valuable design legacy . . . Albrecht, *Designing Dreams: Modern Architecture in the Movies*, p. 100.

CHAPTER FIVE: MGM MODERNE

77. *Part of the fascination of the style* . . . Benton, *Art Deco: 1910–1939*, p. 13.
78. *The new lights work many reversals* . . . *New York News*, March 25, 1928, n.p.
   Bad colds and similar complaints . . . *NY Daily Review*, April 14, 1928, n.p.
79. *The sets are ultra-modernistic* . . . *Orlando Evening Star*, September 12, 1928, p. 4.
   Modernistic effects in furniture . . . New York Daily Mirror, September 18, 1928, n.p.
   If you are looking for . . . *Los Angeles Times*, October 1, 1928, p. 23.
89. *Really, the architecture is splendid* . . . Metro-Goldwyn-Mayer Exhibitor Pressbook, *Our Modern Maidens*, p. 4.
91. *The settings of major productions* . . . Ibid., p. 4.
   We extend to you . . . Academy of Motion Picture Arts and Sciences Center for Motion Picture Study, Special Collections, Cedric Gibbons Contracts Folder.
92. *Use of the moderne style* . . . Massey, *Hollywood Behind the Screen*, p. 75.
   Some time ago . . . Upholsterer and Interior Decorator, May 1934, p. 112.
93. *Under Gibbons's leadership* . . . Albrecht, p. 98.
   There was not a single timber . . . Metro-Goldwyn-Mayer Exhibitor Pressbook, *Susan Lenox: Her Fall and Rise*, p. 5.
96. *We made everything as attractive* . . . Ibid., p. 5.
100. *Perhaps the consummate expression* . . . Schatz, *The Genius of the System*, p. 108.
103. *On* Grand Hotel . . . *Film Pictorial*, August 1933, n.p.
104. *For pity's sake* . . . *Los Angeles Times*, May 22, 1932, p. 3.
105. Grand Hotel *is no mere setting* . . . Merrick, *Great Falls Montana Tribune*, February 21, 1932, p. 1.
106. *The circular motif acts as a pivot* . . . Albrecht, p. 140.
107. *The greatest discretion must be observed* . . . *American Cinematographer*, February 1932, p. 30.

CHAPTER SIX: EVERY STAGE A HOME

109. *When a woman selects her clothes* . . . *Ladies' Home Journal*, July 1933, p. 25.
110. *A home has much the same decorating problems* . . . Ibid., p. 25.
112. *It achieved an all-time high* . . . *Screen and Radio Weekly*, February 2, 1936, n.p.
115. *Comes a long stride* . . . Metro-Goldwyn-Mayer Exhibitor Pressbook, *Should Ladies Behave*, p. 4.
   Most of the furniture . . . Ibid., p. 4.

116. *Witness the entrance of a fresh note* . . . *The Vancouver Sun*, November 10, 1934, p. 9.
117. *Ultra-smartness, refinement, and dignity* . . . Metro-Goldwyn-Mayer Exhibitor Pressbook, *Chained*, p. 5.
    Strange as it may seem . . . Ibid., p. 5.
123. *In designing the sets for* The Women . . . Willis, *Oakland Tribune*, September 27, 1939, p. D-3.
125. *The handsome mantles [sic]* . . . Ibid., p. D-3.
129. *It sounds like a ghastly combination* . . . Metro-Goldwyn-Mayer Exhibitor Pressbook, *Dinner at Eight*, p. 6.
130. *It was a period when dark woods* . . . Metro-Goldwyn-Mayer Exhibitor Pressbook, *After the Thin Man*, p. 6.
    Those sets are an example . . . Lambert, *On Cukor*, p. 181.
132. *The film's sets were exceptionally beautiful* . . . Higham and Greenberg, eds., *The Celluloid Muse: Hollywood Directors Speak*, p. 68.
135. *Cedric Gibbons and Ed Willis* . . . *House Beautiful*, July/August 1942, p. 36.
    I am enclosing a paste-up of an article . . . Letter from Elizabeth Gordon to Cedric Gibbons dated May 27, 1942, Academy of Motion Picture Arts and Sciences Center for Motion Picture Study, Special Collections, Collection 512, Cedric Gibbons and Hazel Brooks Papers, 1918–1992.
136. *I love* The Women *with Norma Shearer* . . . *House Beautiful*, November 2004, p. 74.

CHAPTER SEVEN: RE-CREATING THE WORLD FOR MGM

137. *We can't cater to a handful of people* . . . Marx, *Mayer and Thalberg: The Make-Believe Saints*, p. 83.
138. *A scholar of some distinction* . . . Kennedy, *Collier's*, April 1, 1933, p. 47.
140. *Otherwise, all would be well* . . . *Oakland Tribune*, June 16, 1935, p. 76.
141. *The classics have more than tripled the demand* . . . Ibid., p. 4.
    No, you would certainly not recognize my prison . . . Metro-Goldwyn-Mayer Exhibitor Pressbook, *The Barretts of Wimpole Street*, p. 7.
142. *The sketches she made proved invaluable* . . . Swenson, *Greta Garbo: A Life Apart*, p. 303.
    Metro was the best studio . . . Ibid., p. 303.
143. *To build the HMS* Bounty . . . Metro-Goldwyn-Mayer Exhibitor Pressbook, *Mutiny on the Bounty*, p. 3.
144. *The stone used in construction was "aged"* . . . Metro-Goldwyn-Mayer Exhibitor Pressbook, *Queen Christina*, p. 7.
147. *Historic, architectural gems that dot the South* . . . Metro-Goldwyn-Mayer Exhibitor Pressbook, *The Gorgeous Hussy*, p. 4.
151. *I have enclosed invoice of first shipment of goods* . . . Letter from Hugh Hunt to Cedric Gibbons dated May 23, 1937, Academy of Motion Picture Arts and Sciences Center for Motion Picture Study, Special Collections, Folder 42, MGM Property Department Files.
152. *The fulfillment of a long-cherished dream* . . . Vieira, *Irving Thalberg: Boy Wonder to Producer Prince*, p. 334.
    The masses don't understand Shakespeare . . . Ibid., p. 338.
154. *Bucknall discovered information* . . . *Oakland Tribune*, October 26, 1935, p. 4.
155. *Architects usually date the Renaissance* . . . "Notes on the Design of Motion Picture Settings for Romeo and Juliet," in *Romeo and Juliet: A Motion Picture Edition Illustrated with Photographs*. New York: Random House, 1936, pp. 253–257.
    Some critics felt that Messel's romantic vision . . . Messel, ed., *In the Theater of Design*, p. 230.

158. *Well, it looks like* . . . Harrison, *Arizona Republic*, April 24, 1938, p. 39.
     He was dead, but it was still his . . . Lambert, *Norma Shearer: A Life*, p. 99.
160. *Taken from construction department requisitions* . . . Academy of Motion Picture Arts and Sciences Center for Motion Picture Study, Special Collections, Art Department Records, Folder 65, Set Construction Costs.
     The picture would have to be done . . . Laura Winston Van Dyke, *Van Dyke and the Mythical City Hollywood*, p. 379.
163. *For his part* . . . Crisler, p. X5.
164. *No doubt Versailles held some special charm for him* . . . Mitford, *The Sun King*, p. 20.
165. *One of our odd problems* . . . Metro-Goldwyn-Mayer Exhibitor Pressbook, *Camille*, p. 5.
166. *The cottage is 16 kilometers from Versailles* . . . Ibid., p. 5.
168. *A farm would be approached* . . . Brownlow, *Historical Journal of Film, Radio, and Television*. Volume 1, Issue 1, 1989, p. 81.
169. *Gibbons discovered a complete set* . . . Kiesling, *Talking Pictures: How They Are Made, How to Appreciate Them*, p. 84.

CHAPTER EIGHT: THE METRO MUSICALS

171. *With great fanfare, two soundproof stages* . . . *The Broadway Melody*, Metro-Goldwyn-Mayer, 1929, Souvenir Program, Collection of The New York Public Library for the Performing Arts.
172. *Building sets of proper acoustic material* . . . Fischer, *Art Direction and Production Design*, p. 51.
     That's not a motion picture . . . Thomas, p. 110.
     This is an experiment . . . Ibid., p. 110.
175 *A movie set should never talk* . . . Metro-Goldwyn-Mayer Exhibitor Pressbook, *Our Modern Maidens*, p. 4
180. *Ziegfeld wouldn't have done that* . . . Spiro, *Screen and Radio Weekly*, p. 8.
     A massive spiral volute . . . Metro-Goldwyn-Mayer Exhibitor Pressbook, *The Great Ziegfeld*, p. 4.
183. *A scenic flash that makes the editor wonder* . . . Review: *The Great Ziegfeld*, *Variety*, April 15, 1936, n.p.
     You would get with the art director . . . Kobal, *People Will Talk*, p. 228.
     There are seven sets . . . Metro-Goldwyn-Mayer Exhibitor Pressbook, *Born to Dance*, p. 5.
188. *His camera never quit moving* . . . Reid, "We Cover the Studios," *Photoplay*, January 1938, p. 45.
     The world's largest and heaviest curtain . . . Metro-Goldwyn-Mayer Exhibitor Pressbook, *Broadway Melody of 1938*, p. 6.
189. *Each design was made into a model* . . . Metro-Goldwyn-Mayer Exhibitor Pressbook, *The Wizard of Oz*, p. 8.
190. *Ordinarily, you could go to a book* . . . Harmetz, *The Making of* The Wizard of Oz, p. 212.
     He found a tiny, really miniscule photograph . . . Ibid., p. 215.
     The first glimpse of the exterior . . . Ibid., p. 211.
193. *For your information* . . . Academy of Motion Picture Arts and Sciences Center for Motion Picture Study. Special Collections. Folder 18.   MGM Art Department/E.J. Mannix File.
194. *A "medieval fiefdom"* . . . Patrick Downing and John Hambley, *The Art of Hollywood: Fifty Years of Art Direction*, p. 59.
     I had problems with the MGM art department . . . Greenburg and Higham, p. 199.
     I was always being called on the carpet . . . Donald Knox, *The Magic Factory: How MGM Made An American in Paris*, p. 116.
     Vincente Minnelli is a very unique individual . . . Delamater, *Dance in the Hollywood Musical*, pp. 235–236.

When communicating with Minnelli . . . Hugh Fordin, *The World of Entertainment*, p. 22.

Cedric Gibbons had an idea of doing it one way . . . Knox, p. 22.

195. *Minnelli believed more in beauty . . . .* Sarris, *You Ain't Heard Nothin' Yet*, p. 55.

196. *The visual aspect has always been important . . .* Garaycochea and Serebrinsky, *Movie*, June 1962, p. 24.

Scarcely a branch of film production . . . Fischer, p. 71.

I want to make this into . . . Fordin, p. 94.

The new "St. Louis Street" . . . Academy of Motion Picture Arts and Sciences Center for Motion Picture Study, Special Collections, Art Department Records, Folder 65, Set Construction Costs.

197. *The décor of* Meet Me in St. Louis *. . .* Joseph Andrew Casper, *A Critical Study of the Film Musicals of Vincente Minnelli*, p. 236.

200. *An iridescent, shimmering, supernatural . . . "* Fordin, p. 141.

201. *They poured out like lava from a volcano . . .* Ibid., p 142.

You've got to remember . . . Ibid., p. 142.

202. *Mr. Duell, if that set wasn't big and white before . . .* Academy of Motion Picture Arts and Sciences Center for Motion Picture Study, Special Collections, Collection 512, Cedric Gibbons and Hazel Brooks Papers, 1918–1992.

Let's bring it back to Earth . . . Delamater, p. 255.

204. *In those days, we spent every nickel we could . . .* Ibid., p. 242.

Often times, Gene [Kelly] didn't have the budget . . . Ibid., p. 247.

When you talk about the Caribbean . . . Ibid., p.256.

207. *A real 'carny' kind of look to it . . .* Ibid., p. 239.

He's one of the reasons . . . MGM Art Department Records Folder 33/Personnel Contract Data, 1948–1956.

208. *Oliver took a look at me . . .* Fordin, p. 403.

Minnelli once retorted . . . Harvey, *Directed by Vincente Minnelli*, p. 16.

The studio at that time had a tremendous backlog . . . Delamater, p. 250.

209. *They didn't want to spend a lot of money . . .* Ibid., pp. 245–246.

210. *We never went outdoors once . . .* Ibid., pp. 240–241.

212. *There is a certain thinking today . . .* Ibid., p. 242.

213. *He felt, and rightly so . . .* Donald Knox, *The Magic Factory: How MGM Made* An American in Paris, p. 4.

Well, Minnelli says to me . . . Ibid., p. 15.

214. *In the meetings . . .* Ibid., p. 59.

Okay, on a stage we'll create Notre Dame . . . Ibid., p. 60.

Have you ever danced on cobblestones? . . . Fordin, p. 312.

215. *Every day I would see Minnelli . . .* Knox, p. 62.

There were certain things that I wanted to do . . . Ibid., p. 101.

216. *The director threw up his arms in horror! . . .* Ibid., p. 125.

218. *They couldn't appreciate the fact . . .* Knox, p. 198.

CHAPTER NINE: A MODERNE LOVE STORY

222. *She's cold and rather lifeless . . .* Hunt, p. 75.

Suddenly a wave of silence enveloped the scene . . . Ibid., p. 135.

223. *Only the altar lights . . . Oshkosh Daily Northwestern*, Oshkosh, WI, August 7, 1930, page 9.

It seems strange to be writing you . . . Dolores del Rio papers, Letters, 1930–1939, National Autonomous University of Mexico.

227. *The whole house is an essay* . . . Goldberger, *New York Times*, November 6, 1980, p. C10.
228. *The floor plan by itself is intriguing* . . . Ibid., p. C10.
    In this startling house . . . Calhoun, *Motion Picture*, November 1934, p. 48.
    It was planned and built . . . Ibid., p. 88.
234. *We live like lovers—deliberately* . . . *Modern Screen*, July 1935, n.p.
235. *A certain type of Hollywood glamour* . . . Goldberger, p. C11.

EPILOGUE

238. *In 1927 and 1928 there were exhibitions* . . . Friedman, *Making America Modern*, p. 13.
239. *Stories abound of Gibbons* . . . Downing and Hambley, *The Art of Hollywood*, p. 54.
    "Dear Gibby," it read, "it gives us pleasure . . ." Card to Cedric Gibbons from Hans Peters, Buddy Gillespie, George Gibson, Preston Ames, Edward Carfagno, and Merrill Pye, Academy of Motion Picture Arts and Sciences Center for Motion Picture Study, Special Collections, Collection 512, Cedric Gibbons and Hazel Brooks Papers, 1918–1992.
    Continued to mythologize Gibbons's past . . . *Cleveland Plain Dealer*, October 14, 1951, p. 38-D.
    The considerable wealth of his family . . . *Hollywood Studio Magazine*, November 1956, n.p.
240. *Gibbons and those people didn't care about realism* . . . Boyle, *Los Angeles Times*, November 9, 1986, p. 23.
    At Metro, at that time . . . Delamater, p. 532.
241. *The distinct Metro style was set up by Cedric Gibbons* . . . Chierichetti, *Mitchell Leisen: Hollywood Director*, pp. 219–220.
243. *Decorators have told me* . . . Willis, *Los Angeles Times*, April 16, 1941, Part IV, p. 8.
245. *Like a lot of people* . . . Long, *George Cukor: Interviews*, p. 7.
    The American cinema is a classical art . . . Schatz, p. xiii.
    The estimate that Gibbons made for the cost . . . MGM Art Department Records, Folder 65, Set Construction Costs.
246. *All of the art department* . . . Ibid.
    Gentlemen: This is to inform you . . . MGM Art Department Records, Folder 35, Contracts.
    To get authentic settings . . . Metro-Goldwyn-Mayer Exhibitor Pressbook, *Somebody Up There Likes Me*, p. 6.
247. *In the United States* . . . Affron, *Sets in Motion: Art Direction and Film Narrative*, p. 2.
248. *How much do we hear?* . . . *Los Angeles Times*, May 4, 1970, Part 1, p. 3.
    The beauty of Cedric Gibbons . . . Knox, p. 30.
    There are no schools turning out . . . Elmer Gray, *Pencil Points*, Volume XVI, No. 1, January 1935, p. 33.
249. *On the evening of June 8, 1950* . . . Academy of Motion Picture Arts and Sciences Center for Motion Picture Study, Special Collections, Collection 512, Cedric Gibbons and Hazel Brooks Papers, 1918–1992.
    The following telegrams of congratulations . . . Ibid.
    I have been told that . . . Ibid.

BIBLIOGRAPHY

BOOKS

Affron, Charles, and Mirella Jona. *Sets in Motion: Art Direction and Film Narrative*. New Brunswick, NJ: Rutgers University Press.

Albrecht, Donald. *Designing Dreams: Modern Architecture in the Movies*. New York: Harper Collins, 1986.

Balio, Tino. *Grand Design: Hollywood as a Modern Business Enterprise*. Los Angeles: University of California Press, 1993.

Ballin, Hugo. *Mural Paintings*. New York: Private Printing, 1913.

Barsacq, Léon. *Caligari's Cabinet and Other Grand Illusions: A History of Film Design*. Boston: New York Graphic Society, 1976.

Battersby, Martin. *The Decorative Thirties*. New York: Watson-Guptill Publications, 1988.

Benton, Charlotte, and Tim Benton, Ghislaine Wood, and Oriana Baddeley. *Art Deco 1910–1939*. New York: Bullfinch, 2003.

Berg, A. Scott, *Goldwyn: A Biography*. New York: Alfred A. Knopf, 1989.

Bingen, Steven, Stephen X. Sylvester, and Michael Troyan. *MGM: Hollywood's Greatest Backlot*. Solana Beach, CA: Santa Monica Press, 2011.

Brownlow, Kevin. *The Parade's Gone By*. Los Angeles: University of California Press, 1968.

Brownstein, Elizabeth Smith. *If This House Could Talk*. New York: Simon & Schuster, 1999.

Casper, Joseph Andrew. *Vincente Minnelli and the Film Musical*. New York: A. S. Barnes, 1977.

Castle, Charles. *Oliver Messel: A Biography*. London: Thames and Hudson, 1986.

Chierichetti, David. *Mitchell Leisen: Hollywood Director*. Los Angeles: Photoventures Co., 1995.

Crowther, Bosley. *The Lion's Share*. New York: Dutton, 1957.

Delamater, Jerome. *Dance in the Hollywood Musical*. Ann Arbor, MI: UMI Research Press, 1981.

Everson, William K. *American Silent Film*. New York: Oxford University Press, 1978.

Eyman, Scott. *Empire of Dreams: The Epic Life of Cecil B. DeMille*. New York: Simon & Schuster, 2010.

————. *Lion of Hollywood: The Life and Legend of Louis B. Mayer.* New York: Simon & Schuster, 2012.

————. *The Speed of Sound: Hollywood and the Talkie Revolution.* New York: Simon & Schuster, 1997.

Fales, Winnifred. *What's New in Home Decorating.* New York: Dodd, Mead and Company, 1936.

Fischer, Lucy, ed. *Art Direction and Production Design.* New Brunswick, NJ: Rutgers University Press, 2015.

Flamini, Roland. Irving Thalberg: The Last Tycoon and the World of MGM. New York: Crown Publishers, 1994.

Fordin, Hugh. *The World of Entertainment: Hollywood's Greatest Musicals.* New York: Doubleday, 1975.

Fox, Stanley. *The Mirror Makers: A History of American Advertising and Its Creators.* New York: William Morrow & Co. 1984.

Friedman, Marilyn. *Making America Modern: Interior Design in the 1930s.* Brooklyn, NY: Bauer and Dean, 2018.

Gerstner, David. "Queer Modernism: The Cinematic Aesthetic of Vincente Minnelli." In *Vincente Minnelli: The Art of Entertainment*, edited by Joseph McElhaney. Detroit, MI: Wayne State University Press, 2008.

Gibbons, Cedric. "Notes on the Design of Motion Picture Settings for *Romeo and Juliet*." In *Romeo and Juliet by William Shakespeare: A Motion Picture Edition Illustrated with Photographs*, edited by Irving G. Thalberg, George Cukor, and Talbot Jennings, 253–57. New York: Random House, 1936.

Goldwyn, Samuel. *Behind the Screen.* New York: George H. Doran Company, 1923.

Greenberg, Joel, and Charles Higham. *The Celluloid Muse: Hollywood Directors Speak.* New York: Signet, 1972.

Hall, Linda B. *Dolores del Rio: Beauty in Light and Shade.* Stanford, CA: Stanford University Press, 2013.

Hambley, John, and Patrick Downing. *The Art of Hollywood: Fifty Years of Art Direction.* London: Thames Television Exhibition Catalog, 1979.

Harmetz, Aljean. *The Making of the Wizard of Oz.* Chicago: Chicago Review Press, 2013.

Harrison, Louis Reeves. *Screencraft.* New York: Chalmers Publishing Company, 1916.

Harvey, Stephen. *Directed by Vincente Minnelli.* New York: Harper and Row, 1989.

Heisner, Beverly. *Art Direction in the Days of the Great Studios.* Jefferson, NC: McFarland Publishing, 2011.

Higham, Charles. *Cecil B. DeMille*. New York: Scribner's, 1973.

Holli, Melvin, and Peter d'A. Jones. *Ethnic Chicago: A Multicultural Portrait*. Grand Rapids, MI: Eerdman's Publishing, 1995.

Jackson, Kenneth T., ed. *Empire City: New York through the Centuries*. New York: Columbia University Press, 2002.

Kiesling, Barrett. *Talking Pictures: How They Are Made, How to Appreciate Them*. New York: Johnson Publishers, 1937.

Knox, Donald. *The Magic Factory: How MGM Made* An American in Paris. Westport, CT: Praeger Publishing, 1973.

Kobal, John. *People Will Talk*. New York: Alfred A Knopf, 1986.

Koszarski, Richard. *An Evening's Entertainment: The Silent Feature 1915–1928*. New York: Scribner's, 1990.

Lambert, Gavin. *Norma Shearer: A Life*. New York: Alfred A. Knopf, 1990.

———. *On Cukor*. New York: Rizzoli, 2000.

Landgren, Marshal E. *Years of Art: The Story of the Art Students League of New York*. New York: Robert M. McBride and Company, 1940.

LoBiutto, Vincent. *The Filmmakers Guide to Production Design*. New York: Allworth Press, 2002.

Long, Robert Emmet, ed. *George Cukor: Interviews*. Jackson: University of Mississippi Press, 2001.

Mandelbaum, Howard, and Eric Myers. *Forties Screen Style: A Celebration of High Pastiche in Hollywood*. Santa Monica, CA: Hennessey and Ingalls, 2000.

———. *Screen Deco: A Celebration of High Style in Hollywood*. Santa Monica, CA: Hennessey and Ingalls, 2000.

Marx, Samuel. *Mayer and Thalberg: The Make-Believe Saints*. New York: Random House, 1975.

Massey, Anne. *Hollywood beyond the Screen: Design and Material Culture*. Oxford, England: Berg Publishers, 2000.

McCullough, David W. *Brooklyn: And How It Got That Way*. New York: Dial Press, 1983.

Messel, Thomas, ed. *Oliver Messel: In the Theater of Design*. New York, Rizzoli, 2011.

Mitford, Nancy. *The Sun King*. New York: HarperCollins, 1966.

Moffitt, John F., and Juan Antonio Ramírez. *Architecture for the Screen: A Critical Study of Set Design in Hollywood's Golden Age*. Jefferson, NC: McFarland Publishing Company, 2004.

Naumburg, Nancy. *We Make the Movies*. New York: W. W. Norton, 1937.

Sanders, James. *Celluloid Skyline: New York and the Movies*. New York: Alfred A. Knopf, 2001.

Sarris, Andrew. *The American Cinema: Directors and Directions 1929–1968*. London: Octagon Books, 1982.

———. *You Ain't Heard Nothin' Yet: The American Talking Film, History and Memory, 1927–1949*. New York: Oxford University Press, 1989.

Schatz, Thomas. *The Genius of the System: Hollywood Filmmaking in the Studio Era*. New York: Pantheon Books, 1988.

Sennett, Robert S. *Setting the Scene: The Great Hollywood Art Directors*. New York: Harry N. Abrams, 1994.

Shiel, Mark. *Hollywood Cinema and the Real Los Angeles*. London: Reaktion Books, 2012.

Slide, Anthony. *Early American Cinema*. Metuchen, NJ: Scarecrow Press, 1994.

Solomon, Joe. *Ben-Hur: The Original Blockbuster*. Edinburgh: Edinburgh University Press, 2016.

Stephens, Michael. *Art Directors in Cinema: A Worldwide Biographical Dictionary*. Jefferson, NC: McFarland Publishing Company, 1998.

Swenson, Karen. *Garbo: A Life Apart*. New York: Scribner's, 1997.

Thomas, Bob. *Thalberg: Life and Legend*. New York: Double, 1969.

Tungate, Mark. *Adland: A Global History of Advertising*. London: Kogan Page Publishing, 2013.

Urban, Joseph. "The Cinema Designer Confronts Sound." In *Revolt in the Arts*, edited by Oliver M. Sayler, 241–44. New York: Brentano's, 1930.

Van Dyke, Laura Winston. *Van Dyke and the Mythical City Hollywood*. Culver City, CA: Murray and Gee Publishers, 1948.

Vieira, Mark. *Thalberg: Boy Wonder to Producer Prince*. Los Angeles: University of California Press, 2009.

Watts, Stephen, ed. *Behind the Screen: How Films Are Made*. London: Arthur Barker, 1938.

Whitlock, Cathy. *Designs on Film*. New York: HarperCollins, 2010.

SIGNED ARTICLES

Anderson, Antony. "The New Art of the Studio." *Los Angeles Times*, April 27, 1919, part 3, p. 1.

Ballin, Hugo. "The Scenic Background." *Mentor 9* (July 1921): 22–28.

Barnes, Sanford D. "The Cinema Architect." *American Architect*, February 14, 1923, 169–72.

Bernhard, Lucien. "*House and Garden*'s Modern House." *House and Garden*, January 1929, 60–62.

Blakeston, Oswell. "The Films in Pictorial Review." *Architectural Review*, March 1933, 127.

Brownlow, Kevin. "Ben Carré." *Sight and Sound* 49, no. 1 (Winter, 1979/80): 49–50.

———. "Sydney Franklin and The Good Earth." *Historical Journal of Film, Radio, and Television* 1, no. 1 (1989): 81–82.

Buckland, Wilfred. "The Coming Revolution in Scenic Art." *Harper's Weekly*, March 25, 1916, 306–7.

———. "The Scenic Side of the Photodrama." *Moving Picture World*, July 21, 1917, 439.

Calhoun, Dorothy. "As Modern as Tomorrow . . . Dolores del Rio's Home." *Motion Picture*, November 1934, 48–49, 87–88.

Carrick, Edward. "Moving Picture Sets—A Medium for the Architect." *Architectural Record*, May 1930, 440–44.

Chrisler, B. R. "Dolores and Husband: Interview with Cedric Gibbons." *New York Times*, February 6, 1938, 5.

Cohn, Alfred A. "The Art Director." *Photoplay*, August 1916, 43–46, 177.

Corliss, Mary, and Carlos Clarens. "Architecture and the Motion Picture." *Film Comment*, May/June 1978, 25–58.

Cummings, Mitzi. "She Walks in Beauty." *Photoplay*, March 1938, 32, 78, 80.

Deschner, Donald. "Edward Carfagno, MGM Art Director." *Velvet Light Trap*, no. 18 (Spring 1978): 30–34.

Dillon, Carmen "The Art Director." *Films and Filming,* May 1937,

Draper, Muriel. "Modern Modes in Furniture: The Multiform Shapes of Machinery Influence Our Newest Furniture." *Harper's Bazaar*, March 1928, 98–99.

Erengis, George P. "Cedric Gibbons: Set a Standard for Art Direction that Raised the Movies' Cultural Level," *Films in Review*, April 1965, 217–32.

———. "MGM's Backlot." *Films in Review,* April 1965, 23–37.

Eustis, Morton. "Designing for the Movies: Gibbons of MGM." *Theater Arts,* October 1932, 782–98.

Fidler, Jimmy. "Jimmy Fidler in Hollywood." *Los Angeles Times,* June 21, 1941, section C, part B, p. 3.

Field, Alice Evans. "The Art Director's Art." *Films in Review,* February 1952.

Flint, Ralph. "Cedric Gibbons." *Creative Art: A Magazine of Fine and Applied Art,* October 1932, 116–19.

———. "Cinema's Art Directors." *New York Times,* November 22, 1931, n.p.

Gebhart, Myrtle. "She Lives in Beauty." *Picture Play,* November 1937, 64–69, 90.

Gibbons, Cedric. "Motion Picture Sets." In *The Theatre and Motion Pictures: A Selection of Articles from the New 14th Edition of the Encyclopedia Britannica.* New York: Encyclopedia Britannica, 1929, pp. 26–28.

———. "The Set as an Actor." *American Cinematographer,* February 1932, 30.

Gill, Brendan. "Cedric Gibbons and Dolores del Rio: The Art Director and Star of *Flying Down to Rio* in Santa Monica." *Architectural Digest,* April 1992, 128–33, 254.

Goldberger, Paul. "A Hollywood House Worthy of an Oscar." *New York Times,* November 1980, C10.

Gorelick, Mordecai. "Hollywood's Art Machinery." *Hollywood Quarterly,* Autumn 1946, 153–60.

Grant, Jack. "Hollywood's First Art Director." *American Cinematographer,* May 1941, 219, 238.

Harrison, Louis Reeves. "Settings." *Moving Picture World,* June 11, 1911, 1360.

Harrison, Paul. "The Queen Gets Bossed—And Likes It." *Arizona Republic,* August 24, 1938, 39–40.

———. "When the Movies Set the Stage." *Laredo Times,* 1936, n.p.

Harvey, Hope. "Changing Habits in Daily Living." *Woman's Home Companion,* April 1928, 134–35.

Hefferman, Howard. "Modern Home Shouldn't Act." *Baltimore Sun,* June 21, 1953, n.p.

Henderson, Brian. "Notes on Set Design and Cinema." *Film Quarterly,* Fall 1988, 17–20.

Horner, Harry. "Designing for the Screen." *Theatre Arts,* November 1941, 794–98.

Howard, Kathleen. "White Accents." *Harper's Bazaar,* August 1931, 35.

Hunt, Hugh. "Character Set Dressing Is Separate Type of Studio Artistry." *Motion Picture Studio Insider,* May 1935, n.p.

Jackson, J. A. "Photoplay Architecture." *Los Angeles Times*, February 19, 1922, part 8, p. 5.

James, Caryn. "Romanticizing Hollywood's Dream Factory." *New York Times*, November 7, 1989, C17, C24.

Julian, Ralph. "The City of Brooklyn." *Harper's Monthly*, April 1893, 650–71.

Kay, Jane Holtz. "When Hollywood Was Golden, the Movie Sets Were, Too." *New York Times*, January 11, 1990, C12.

Keel, Chester A. "The Fiasco of *Ben-Hur*." *Photoplay*, October 1924, 32–33, 101.

Kennedy, John B. "Hits and Errors." *Collier's*, April 1, 1933, 47.

Kirkpatrick, Diane. "Editor's Statement: Art History and the Study of Film." *Art Journal*, Fall 1983, 221.

Kramer, William M. "Hugo Ballin, A Forgotten Artist of Hollywood—Part 1." *Western States Jewish History*, October 1991, 3–11.

———. "Hugo Ballin, A Forgotten Artist of Hollywood—Part II." *Western States Jewish History*, January 1992, 136–47.

Lachenbruch, Jerome. "Art and Architecture Artifice." *American Architect*, November 3, 1920, 563–68.

Laing, A. B. "Designing Motion Picture Sets." *Architectural Record*, July 1933, 59–64.

Latham, Maude. "Their Homes Reflect Them." *Picture Play*, July 1934.

Lewis, Arnold, and Kevin Lewis. "Include Me Out: Samuel Goldwyn and Joe Godsol." *Film History* 2 (1988): 133–53.

Lindsay, Vachel. "A Plea for the Art World." *Moving Picture World*, July 21, 1917, 368.

Lipke, Katherine. "Lemon-Colored Bathrooms and Trousers for Girl Hikers." *Los Angeles Times*, April 22, 1923, part 3, p. 13.

MacGowan, Kenneth. "Enter the Artist." *Photoplay*, January 1921, 73–75.

———. "The New Studio Art." *Motion Picture Classic*, March 1919, 16–18, 65–66, 74.

Merrick, Mollie. "Greatest Effort in Settings Since Advent of Sound Films Is Expended on *Grand Hotel*." *Great Falls* (Montana) *Tribune*, February 21, 1932, p. 19.

Moses, Vivian M. "With Art as Her Handmaiden." *Moving Picture World*, July 21, 1917, 383–87.

Peak, Mayme Ober. "Every Home's a Stage." *Ladies' Home Journal*, July 1933, 25, 77.

Physioc, Wray Bartlett. "Restraint in Interior Decoration." *Moving Picture World*, May 25, 1912, 714.

Reid, James. "We Cover the Studios." *Photoplay*, January 1938, 44–45.

Rimoldi, Oscar. "Cedric Gibbons: MGM Art Director." *Hollywood Studio Magazine*, March 1990, 11–15.

Schubert, Edwin, and Elza Schubert. "Hollywood High Lights." *Picture Play*, September 1934, 28–29, 59, 63.

Scott, John L. "Film Sets Grow Larger." *Los Angeles Times*, September 1, 1929, 2.

Serebrinsky, Ernesto, and Oscar Garaycochea, "Vincente Minnelli Interviewed in Argentina." *Movie No. 1*, June 1962, 24.

Sexton, R. W. "Good and Bad in Movie Interiors." *Photoplay*, January 1925, 58, 134.

Spiro, J. D. "Hollywood's Musical Splurge." *Screen and Radio Weekly*, August 29, 1936, 8–9.

Sterner, Harold. "An Architect Goes to the Movies." *Arts*, November 1929, 167–68.

Stone, Selma, "Bits about Town," *Twin City News*, August 9, 1939, 24.

Stuart, Betty Thornley. "Movie Set-Up." *Collier's*, September 30, 1933, 20–24.

Thomson, David. "The Art of the Art Director." *American Film*, February 1977, 12–20.

Torgerson, Dial. "Props Become Stars in MGM 'Spectacular.'" *Los Angeles Times*, May 4, 1970, part 1, p. 3.

Tourneur, Maurice. "The Artistry of Motion Pictures." *Moving Picture World*, July 21, 1917, 378–79.

Tully, Judd. "The Art Students League of New York." *American Artist*, August 1984. 52–53.

Untermeyer, Louis. "Hugo Ballin's Decorations for the Capitol at Madison." *Art and Progress*, September 1912, 699–702.

Verk, Stefan. "Designer for the Screen: Cedric Gibbons." *American Artist*, November 1948, 9–10, 38–39, 68–69.

Waterbury, Ruth. "A Modern Miracle Film." *Photoplay*, March 1926, 32, 134.

Whitaker, Alma. "Sets for Grand Hotel 'Act' Out Film's Moods." *Los Angeles Times*, May 22, 1932, p. 3.

Wilcox, Grace. "She's Making a Russian Out of Garbo." *Oakland Tribune*, June 16, 1935, 76.

Willis, Edwin B. "Film Interior Sets Intrigue Homemakers." *Los Angeles Times*, April 16, 1941, part 4, p. 8.

———. "Period Pieces Grace Big Room." *Oakland Tribune*, September 27, 1939, D-3.

———. "Remodeled Country House Has Fine New Features." *Boston Globe*, September 13, 1939, p. 27.

UNSIGNED ARTICLES

"The Architecture of Motion Picture Settings." *The American Architect*, July 7, 1920, 2–5.

"At the Movies: Marshall Neilan's Latest Drama, *The Rendezvous*." *Wichita Daily Times*, February 17, 1924, 23

"Balboa Studio Turned Over to Creditors." *Moving Picture World*, April 21, 1918, 376.

"Cedric Gibbons Heads Art Department at One of Major Studios." *Dayton* (Ohio) *Daily News*, February 27, 1938, section 2, p. 5.

"Crawford and Gable On-Screen in *Chained*." *Ruston Daily Leader*, October 25, 1934, 7.

"Dancing Daughters Has Lavish Setting." *Orlando Evening Star*, September 12, 1928, 4.

"A Day in a Modern Apartment." *Harper's Bazaar*, April 1928, 110–11.

"Day of Lavish Film Settings Is Past." *Great Falls Tribune*, March 9, 1924, 21.

"Dressing the Sets." *Motion Picture*, June 1926, 34–35, 76.

"Duplicate Big Depot in Film." *San Bernardino Daily Sun*, February 10, 1924.

"Everett Shinn Engaged by Goldwyn Pictures Corporation." *Moving Picture World*, May 26, 1917, 1289.

"George Cukor: Interview." *American Film Institute, 1978*, 110–11.

"Getting Belasco Atmosphere: Mr. Wilfred Buckland Engaged by the Jesse L. Lasky Company to Stage Its Future Productions." *Moving Picture World*, May 30, 1914, 1271.

"Goldwyn Buys Triangle Studio." *Motion Picture News*, June 7, 1919, 3811.

"Goldwyn Glass Roof Painted Black." *Moving Picture World*, January–March 1918, 83.

"Goldwyn to Temper the Summer's Heat." *Moving Picture World*, July 20, 1918, 377.

"Grandma's Horsehair Sofa Goes Modern for Smart Sets in *No More Ladies*." *Big Spring Texas Daily Herald*, June 30, 1935, 2.

"Great Joppa Gate Set Built for *Ben-Hur*." *Moving Picture World*, August 16, 1924, 560.

"Has Impressionism Arrived in the Motion Pictures?" *Kansas City Star*, July 3, 1921, 44.

"The Home of Mr. and Mrs. Cedric Gibbons, Santa Monica, California." *California Arts and Architecture*, December 1937, 26–27.

"Meet Director T. Hayes Hunter, the director of *Earthbound*." *Motion Picture News*, September 4, 1920, 1911.

"Movie Art Departments Play Guiding Roles in Film Making." *Cleveland Plain Dealer*, October 14, 1951.

"Movie Facts and Fancies." *Boston Globe*, May 5, 1924, 3.

"New Incandescent Lights Work Color Reversals in Films." *New York Review*, April 14, 1928, n.p.

"New Invention Revolutionizes Motion Picture Scenery." *Scientific American*, July 1922, 23.

"A New York Decorator's Opinion of the Paris Exposition." *Good Furniture Magazine*, October 1925, n.p.

"Opening Day of Earthbound in New York City." *New York Morning Telegraph*, September 20, 1920, n.p.

"Remaking the World for the Movies." *Popular Mechanics*, April 1936, 546–49.

"Review: The Great Ziegfeld." *Variety*, April 15, 1936, n.p.

"The Screen: *Our Dancing Daughters*." *Los Angeles Times*, October 1, 1928, 23.

"The Screen: *When Knighthood Was in Flower*." *New York Times*, September 15, 1922, 17.

"Seeks Verities in Film Settings." *Los Angeles Times*, December 26, 1920, part 3, p. 16.

"Sets of *When Ladies Meet* Broke All Previous Fan Mail Records in 1941." *House Beautiful*, December 1946, 219–20.

"Settings for *Three Weeks*." *Wichita Daily Times*, March 30, 1924, 24.

"Shakespearean Research Jumps." *Oakland Tribune*, October 26, 1935, 4.

"Thalberg Tells Metro Formula of Making Box Office Pictures." *Moving Picture World*, February 7, 1925, 607.

"Today's Top Designers." *House Beautiful*, November 2004, 74.

"Ultra-Modern Sets in Crawford-Gable Film." *Vancouver Sun*, November 10, 1934, 9.

"Wanted: Interior Decorators for the Movies." *House Beautiful*, February 1915, 82.

"What Are Our Plans and What Do We Propose to Do?" *Moving Picture World*, March 1907, 1.

"Why the Movies Are Influencing American Taste." *House Beautiful*, July/August 1942, 36–38.

"Wonders of the Scenic Engineers." *Popular Mechanics*, March 1936, 354–57, 130A.

SPECIAL COLLECTIONS

Academy of Motion Picture Arts and Sciences Center for Motion Picture Study, Special Collections, Art Department Records, Folder 65, Set Construction Costs.

Academy of Motion Picture Arts and Sciences Center for Motion Picture Study, Special Collections, Cedric Gibbons Contracts Folder.

Academy of Motion Picture Arts and Sciences Center for Motion Picture Study, Special Collections, Cedric Gibbons Military Records.

Academy of Motion Picture Arts and Sciences Center for Motion Picture Study, Special Collections, Collection 512, Cedric Gibbons and Hazel Brooks Papers, 1918–1992.

Academy of Motion Picture Arts and Sciences Center for Motion Picture Study, Special Collections, Folder 4, Cedric Gibbons Publicity.

Academy of Motion Picture Arts and Sciences Center for Motion Picture Study, Special Collections, Folder 18, MGM Art Department/E. J. Mannix File.

Academy of Motion Picture Arts and Sciences Center for Motion Picture Study, Special Collections, Folder 35, MGM Art Department Personnel Set Decorators Contracts.

Academy of Motion Picture Arts and Sciences Center for Motion Picture Study, Special Collections, Folder 42, MGM Property Department Files.

Academy of Motion Picture Arts and Sciences Center for Motion Picture Study, Rudy Behlmer Papers, *Ben-Hur*.

Joseph Urban Papers, Rare Book and Manuscript Archive, Columbia University Libraries.

New York City Municipal Archives

Student Records, A. Cedric Gibbons, Art Students League, 215 West 57th Street, New York, NY.

MOTION PICTURE SOUVENIR PROGRAMS

The Broadway Melody, Metro-Goldwyn-Mayer, 1929, Collection of the New York Public Library for the Performing Arts.

Dinner at Eight, Metro-Goldwyn-Mayer, 1933, Collection of the New York Public Library for the Performing Arts.

The Merry Widow, Metro-Goldwyn-Mayer, 1934, Collection of the New York Public Library for the Performing Arts.

PERIODICALS

The American Architect

Bluefield Daily Telegraph

The Bradford Era

Charleston Daily Mail

Collier's

Connersville News Examiner

Creative Art

Cumberland Evening Times

Janesville Daily Gazette

Los Angeles Herald Examiner

Los Angeles Times

The Lowell Sun

Metro-Goldwyn-Mayer Exhibitor Press Books

Morning Telegraph

Motion Picture News

The Moving Picture World

Nevada State Journal

New York News

New York Review

New York Times

Orlando Evening Star

Philadelphia Evening Ledger

Philadelphia Public Ledger

San Antonio Light

Screen and Radio Weekly

Sight and Sound

Syracuse Herald

Theater Arts Monthly

Wichita Daily Times

Winnipeg Free Press

PHOTO CREDITS

Courtesy of the Academy of Motion Picture Arts and Sciences, Metro-Goldwyn-Mayer Collection: Pages vi, xii, xiii, 2, 43, 48, 50, 63, 139, 147, 150 (bottom), 152, 153, 154, 155, 158, 159 (top), 161 (top), 165, 176 (bottom), 178, 179, 181, 191, 192, 217, 224, 227, 228, 229, 231, 236, 241, 242

Courtesy of Photofest, Inc.: xiv, 22, 28 (bottom), 32, 38, 60, 62, 67, 68, 72, 189, 243, 247

Courtesy of the Academy of Motion Picture Arts and Sciences, Metro-Goldwyn-Mayer Set Reference Photos: 94 (top), 95, 97, 98, 102, 103, 104, 105, 114, 115, 116, 118, 119, 121, 122, 124, 126, 128, 131, 132, 133, 134, 140, 142, 143, 145, 146, 148, 150 (top), 159 (bottom), 161 (bottom), 162, 163, 164, 167, 169, 173, 176 (top), 177, 182, 197, 198, 199, 200, 203 (bottom), 205, 209, 211, 212, 216, 244

Courtesy of the Academy of Motion Picture Arts and Sciences, Cedric Gibbons and Hazel Brooks Papers: 111, 112, 156

Courtesy of the Academy of Motion Picture Arts and Sciences, Metro-Goldwyn-Mayer Core Collection Production Files: 120, 123

Courtesy of the Academy of Motion Picture Arts and Sciences, George Cukor Collection: 127

Courtesy of the Academy of Motion Picture Arts and Sciences, Production and Biography Photos: 76, 84, 85, 86, 88, 90, 96, 99, 101, 220, 225, 251

Courtesy of the Academy of Motion Picture Arts and Sciences, Hollywood Museum Collection: 39, 54, 55, 56, 57

Courtesy of the Academy of Motion Picture Arts and Sciences, Herrick Core Collection Production Files: 25, 34, 41, 43, 46, 49, 53, 65, 66, 70, 80, 81, 82, 87, 94 (bottom), 184, 185, 186, 187, 201, 203 (top), 207

Courtesy Scott Frances/OTTO: 226, 230, 233, 234

Courtesy Bison Archives Photographs Collected by Marc Wanamaker: 28 (top)

Courtesy of the Academy of Motion Picture Arts and Sciences, Cecil B. DeMille Collection: 30

INDEX

historical subjects, 138, 143

location filming, 247

merger to form, viii, x, 18, 58

movie lots, ix–xi, xiv, 248

movie sets, ix–xiii, *xii, xiii,* xv, xvi

movie stages, x–xi, xiii, xv, 45, 75, 171–172

musicals, 170, 171–218

property warehouse, 151–152, *152, 153*

real-world locations, 206–207

realism and research department, 138, 144, *159,* 244

requests received for floor plans, costumes, and furniture, xvi, 135, 243

sound stages, xv, 45, 75, 179, 210

soundproof stages, 171

Stock Market crash, 91–92, 100, 108, 113

television and, 204

typical production workflow, 71, 73

MGM musical, 171, 188

Miller, Ann, x–xi, 206

Minnelli, Vincente, 20, 193–197, *195,* 199, *200,* 201–202, 204, 207, 208, 213–218, 245, 250

The Mirror Makers (Fox), 18

Mitford, Nancy, 164

moderne style, 92, 100

Montgomery, Robert, 93, 110, 233

Moore, Jack D., ix

Morgan, Dennis, 180

Morgan, Frank, 110

Moses, Vivian, 39, 40

"The Motiograph!" (projector), 24

Motion Picture Classic (MacGowan), 36

movie sets

  about, ix–xiii

  The American Architect on, 36

applied painting in, 31

architectural approach to set design, 25, *25*

art director's role, 24–36

background in, 26

Ballin on, 15, 39–40, 49–50

Buckland and, 26–27, *28,* 29, 31, 35, 36, 49

Carré and, 13, 14, 30–32, *31*

colored backdrops in, 31, 33, 40

early silent movies, 24–36

Gibbons at Edison Studios, 18, 19

House Beautiful article, 29–30

lighting systems, 27, 29, *30,* 31, 33, 40, 45, 46, 78–79, *164*

modernism and geometrical form in, xv–xvi

outdoor sets, xi

painted scenery, 31, 32

photographic plate enlargements, 31–32

skylines for magical places, 32

Technicolor process, 29, 190

Urban and, 31–34, *33,* 36, 40

use of solid walls and furniture rather than backdrops, 18, 28, 31

The Moving Picture World (magazine), 23, 24, 26, 35

"muddying," 144, *145,* 146

Muni, Paul, 166

Munshin, Jules, 206

Murphy, George, 188

Murray, James, 240, *241, 242*

Murray, Mae, 174

musicals, 170, 171–218

Mutiny on the Bounty (1935), x, 143

Myers, Carmel, 63

The Mystic, 61

Swanson, Gloria, 44

A Tale of Two Cities (1935), xi, 149, *150*
Taylor, Robert, 134
technicolor, 29, 190, 204–206
television, 204
Thalberg, Irving, viii, 58, 59, *60*, 64, 70,
    71, 73, 100, 137, 141, 143, 152, 153,
    154, 158, 165, 166, 168, 170, 172,
    174, 179, 180, 238, 245
theater chains, 57–58, 204
"There's Beauty Everywhere" (song), 200,
    201, 202
The Thin Man (1934), 129
Thomas Edison Studios. *See* Edison
    Studios
Thompson, James Walter, 17
"Thompson T-Square," 17
three-strip technicolor, 190, 206
Three Weeks (1924), 52, 54, *54–56*,
    56, 177
Thurlow, T.H., 136
Tiffany Productions, 4
Time, the Comedian, 61
Tirtoff, Romain de. *See* Erté
Toluboff, Alexander, xv, 74, 93, 96, 100,
    144, 166
Tourneur, Maurice, 13, 31, 35
Tracy, Spencer, 213
The Trail of '98 (1928), 222
Triangle Film Corporation, x, 42
Trilby (1916), 14
Tugboat Annie (1932), x
Tungate, Mark, 17

Untermeyer, Louis, 16
The Unwritten Code (1919), 44
Urban, Joseph, 31–34, *33*, 36, 40

Van, Bobby, xi
Van Dyke, W.S., II, 160, 188
Vera-Ellen, 206
Victorian interior, 130
Vidor, King, 240
Vienna Secession, 32
Viertel, Salka, 144
von Stroheim, Erich, 174

Walters, Charles, 204
Warner Brothers, 19, 75, 174, 182
Warner, Jack, 249
Warren, Harry, 200
Watts, Stephen, xvi
Weidler, Virginia, 122
Weisz, David, 248
What Price Glory? (1926), 222
When Knighthood Was in Flower (1922),
    33, *34*, 138
When Ladies Meet (1933), 110–113,
    111, 112
When Ladies Meet (1941), xvi,
    134–136, 243
Wife vs. Secretary (1936), xii–xiii,
    119–120, *120–123*
Williams, Esther, 206
Willis, Edwin, viii, 73, 74, 113, 120, 123,
    125–126, *128*, 135, 148, 152, *152*,
    160, 165–166, 168, 194, 197, 213,
    243, 248
Wisconsin State Capitol murals, 15–16
The Wizard of Oz (1939), 188–190, *189*,
    191, 192, *192*, 246
Wolfe, Thomas, 13
A Woman of Affairs, 83, *84, 85*
Woman of the Year (1942), 74
The Women (1939), xvi, 123, *124*,
    125–126, *127*, 136